GLENCOE
MATHEMATICS

W9-BHB-029

Teaching Pre-Algebra with Manipulatives

Mc Graw Hill Glencoe
McGraw-Hill

New York, New York
Columbus, Ohio
Chicago, Illinois
Peoria, Illinois
Woodland Hills, California

Manipulatives

Glencoe offers three types of kits to enhance the use of manipulatives in your Pre-Algebra classroom.

- The **Glencoe Mathematics Overhead Manipulative Resources** contains translucent manipulatives designed for use with an overhead projector.

- The **Glencoe Mathematics Classroom Manipulative Kit** contains classroom sets of frequently used manipulatives in algebra, geometry, measurement, probability, and statistics.

- The **Glencoe Mathematics Student Manipulative Kit** contains an individual set of manipulatives often used in Student Edition activities.

The manipulatives contained in each of these kits are listed on page vi of this booklet.

Each of these kits can be ordered from Glencoe by calling (800) 334-7344.

Glencoe Mathematics Overhead Manipulative Kit	0-07-830593-4
Glencoe Mathematics Classroom Manipulative Kit	0-02-833116-8
Glencoe Mathematics Student Manipulative Kit	0-02-833654-2

Glencoe/McGraw-Hill

A Division of The McGraw·Hill Companies

Send all inquiries to:
Glencoe/McGraw-Hill
8787 Orion Place
Columbus, OH 43240

ISBN: 0-07-827796-5   *Teaching Pre-Algebra with Manipulatives*

1 2 3 4 5 6 7 8 9 10 079 11 10 09 08 07 06 05 04 03 02

Contents

Teacher's Guide to Using
Teaching Pre-Algebra with Manipulatives

The book contains two sections of masters—Easy-to-Make Manipulatives and activities for Pre-Algebra. Tabs help you locate the activities for each chapter. A complete list of manipulatives available in each of the three types of Glencoe Mathematics Manipulative Kits appears on the next page.

Easy-to-Make Manipulatives
The first section of this book contains masters for making your own manipulatives. To make more durable manipulatives, consider using card stock. To make algebra tiles similar to those shown in the Student Edition, have students use markers to color the tiles appropriately or use colored card stock.

You can also make transparencies of frequently used items such as grid paper and number lines.

Activity Masters
Each chapter begins with **Teaching Notes and Overview** that summarizes the activities for the chapter and includes sample answers. There are four types of masters.

Mini-Projects are short projects that enable students to work cooperatively in small groups to investigate mathematical concepts.

Using Overhead Manipulatives provides instructions for the teacher to demonstrate an alternate approach to the concepts of the lesson by using manipulatives on the overhead projector.

Student Recording Sheets accompany the Algebra Activities found in the Student Edition. Students can easily record the results of the activity on prepared grids, charts, and figures.

Algebra Activities provide additional activities to enrich the students' experiences. These masters often include a transparency master to accompany the activity.

Glencoe Mathematics Manipulatives

Glencoe Mathematics Overhead Manipulative Resources
ISBN: 0-07-830593-4

Transparencies		Overhead Manipulatives
integer mat	centimeter grid	algebra tiles
equation mat	number lines	spinners
product mat	lined paper	two-dimensional cups
inequality mat	regular polygons	red and yellow counters
dot paper	polynomial models	decimal models (base-ten blocks)
isometric dot paper	integer models	compass
coordinate grids	equation models	protractor
		geoboard/geobands
		geometric shapes
		transparency pens in 4 colors

Glencoe Mathematics Classroom Manipulative Kit
ISBN: 0-02-833116-8

Algebra	Measurement, Probability, and Statistics	Geometry
algebra tiles	base-ten models	compasses
counters	marbles	geoboards
cups	measuring cups	geobands
centimeter cubes	number cubes	geomirrors
equation mat/product mat	protractors	isometric dot grid stamp
coordinate grid stamp and	rulers	pattern blocks
ink pad	scissors	tangrams
	spinners	
	stopwatches	
	tape measures	

Glencoe Mathematics Student Manipulative Kit
ISBN: 0-02-833654-2

algebra tiles	protractor
red and yellow counters	scissors
cups	geoboard
equation /product mat	geobands
compass/ruler	tape measure

Grid Paper

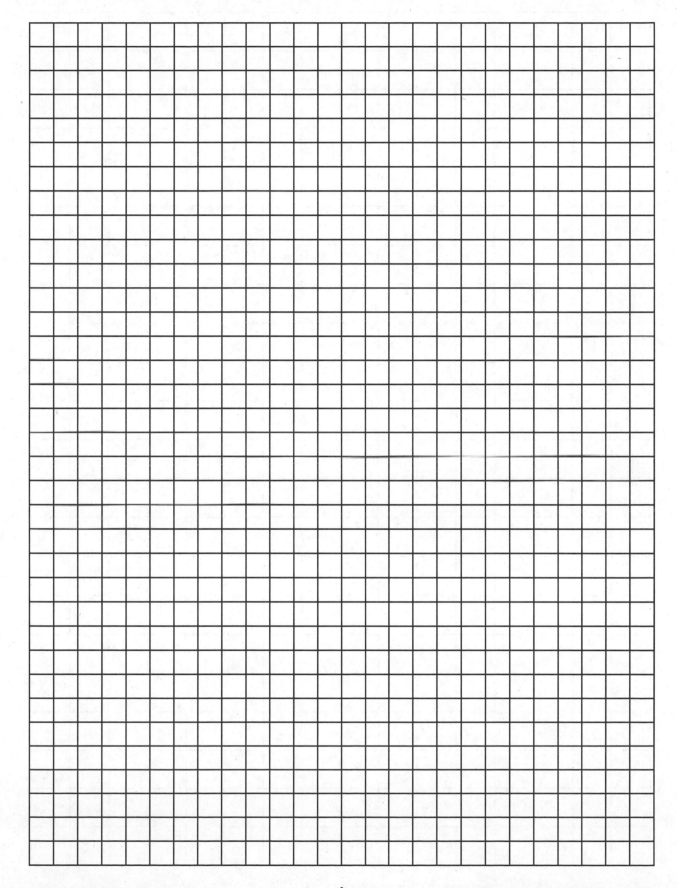

Centimeter Grid Paper

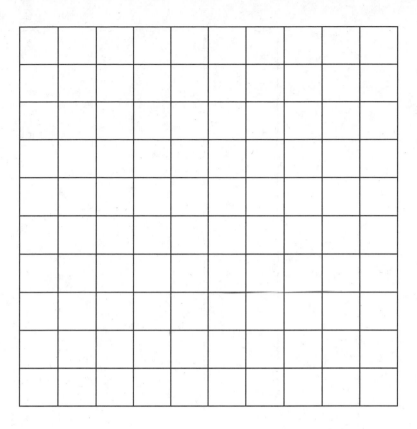

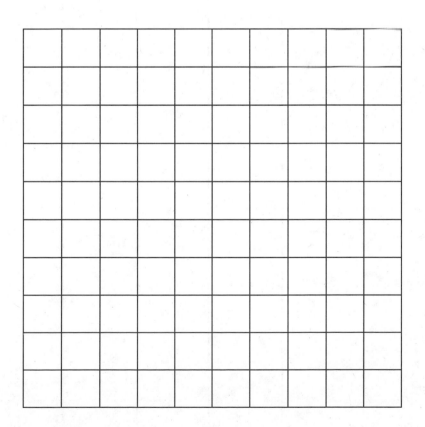

Number Lines

First Quadrant Grids

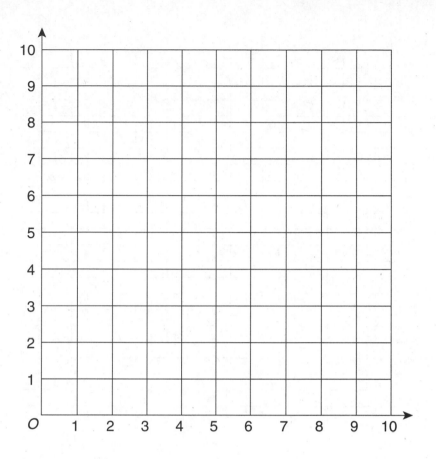

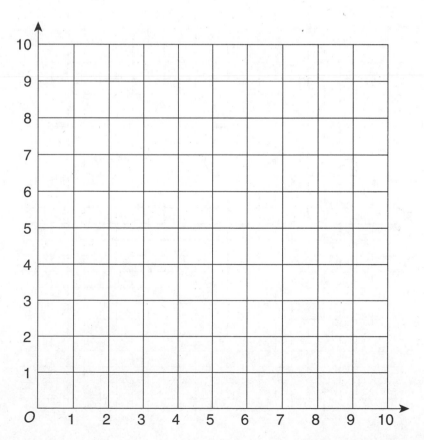

Teaching Pre-Algebra with Manipulatives

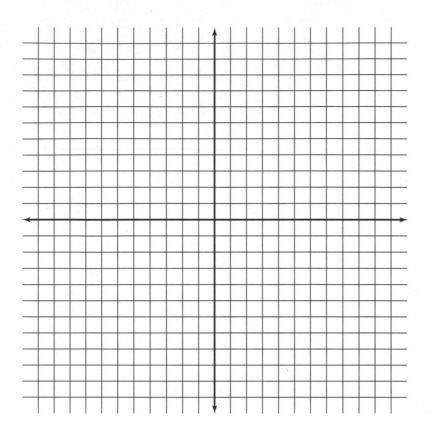

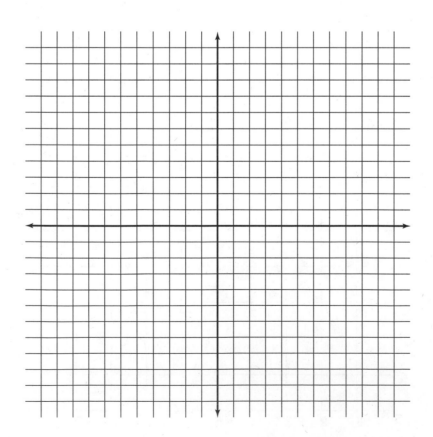

1	1	1	1	1	1	1	1	1	1
1	1	1	1	1	1	1	1	1	1
1	1	1	1	1	1	1	1	1	1
1	1	1	1	1	1	1	1	1	1
1	1	1	1	1	1	1	1	1	1
1	1	1	1	1	1	1	1	1	1
1	1	1	1	1	1	1	1	1	1
−1	−1	−1	−1	−1	−1	−1	−1	−1	−1
−1	−1	−1	−1	−1	−1	−1	−1	−1	−1
−1	−1	−1	−1	−1	−1	−1	−1	−1	−1
−1	−1	−1	−1	−1	−1	−1	−1	−1	−1
−1	−1	−1	−1	−1	−1	−1	−1	−1	−1

Algebra Tiles

(variables)

x	x	x	x	x	x	x	x	x	x
x	x	x	x	x	x	x	x	x	x
$-x$	$-x$	$-x$	$-x$	$-x$	$-x$	$-x$	$-x$	$-x$	$-x$
$-x$	$-x$	$-x$	$-x$	$-x$	$-x$	$-x$	$-x$	$-x$	$-x$

x^2	x^2	x^2	x^2	x^2
$-x^2$	$-x^2$	$-x^2$	$-x^2$	$-x^2$

Integer Models Summary

There are two types of integer tiles.

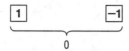

A **zero pair** is formed by pairing one positive integer tile and one negative integer tile.

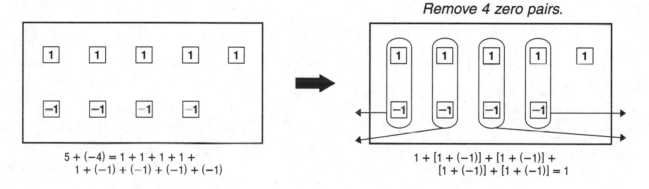

You can remove or add zero pairs to a set without changing the value of the set.

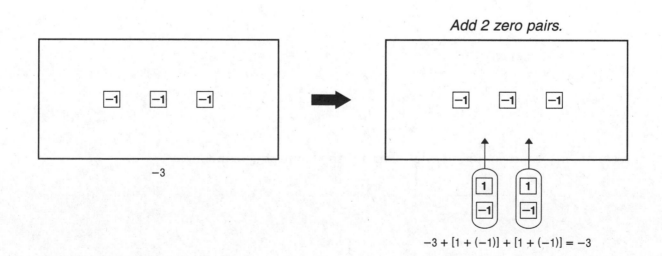

Remove 4 zero pairs.

$5 + (-4) = 1 + 1 + 1 + 1 +$
$1 + (-1) + (-1) + (-1) + (-1)$

$1 + [1 + (-1)] + [1 + (-1)] +$
$[1 + (-1)] + [1 + (-1)] = 1$

Add 2 zero pairs.

-3

$-3 + [1 + (-1)] + [1 + (-1)] = -3$

Polynomial Models Summary

There are three basic tiles used for modeling a polynomial.

$x \cdot x$

$x \cdot 1$

$1 \cdot 1$

Each tile has an opposite.

A **zero pair** results when a tile and its opposite are paired.

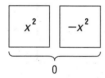

You can add or remove zero pairs to any polynomial without changing its value.

Like terms are represented by tiles that are the same shape and size.

Equation Models Summary

A **zero pair** is formed by pairing one positive tile and one negative tile of the same type.

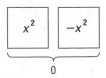

You can remove or add the same number of like tiles to each side of the equation mat.

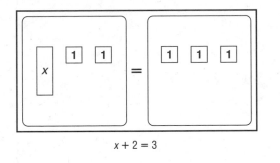

$x + 2 = 3$

Add 2 negative ones to each side.

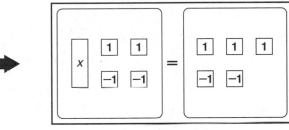

$x + 2 + (-2) = 3 + (-2)$

You can remove or add zero pairs to either side of the equation mat without changing the equation.

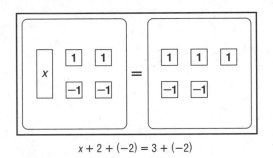

$x + 2 + (-2) = 3 + (-2)$

Remove zero pairs.

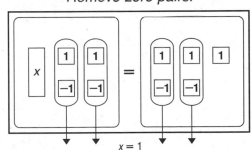

$x = 1$

Rectangular Dot Paper

Isometric Dot Paper

Percent Models

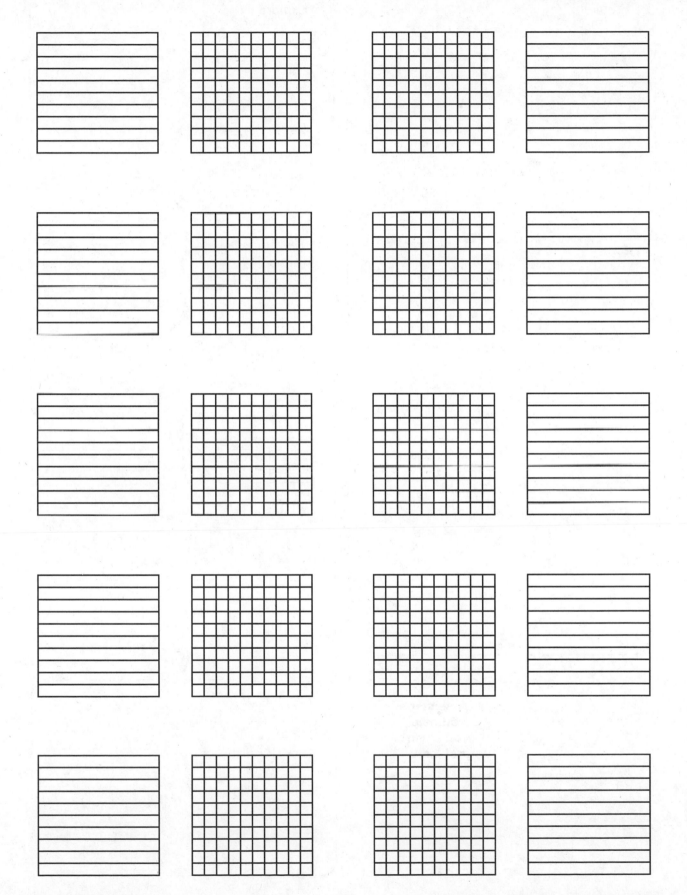

Problem Solving Guide

Problem:

Explore

Plan

Solve

Examine

These steps can help you solve problems.

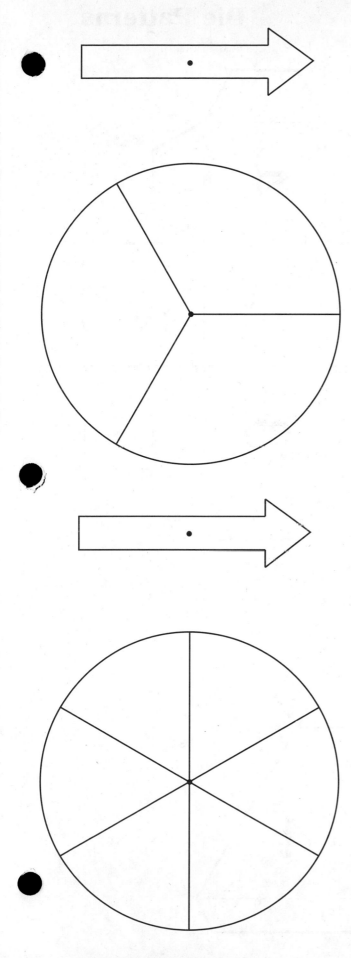

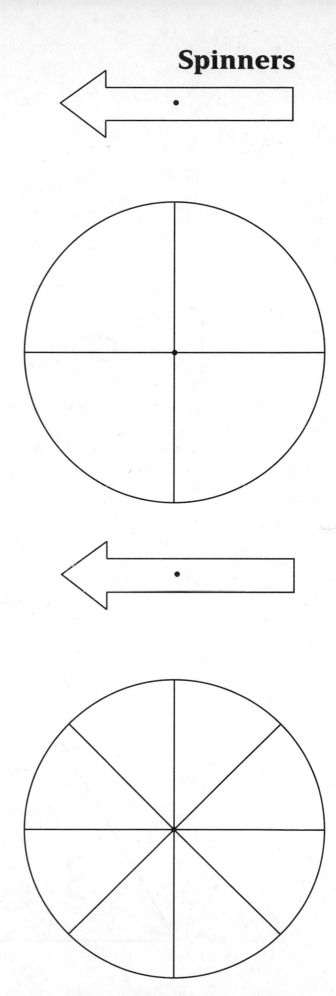

19 *Teaching Pre-Algebra with Manipulatives*

Cut along the heavy black lines.
Fold on the dashed lines.
Tabs can be taped or glued.

Protractors

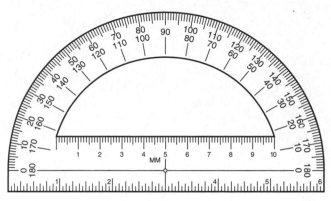

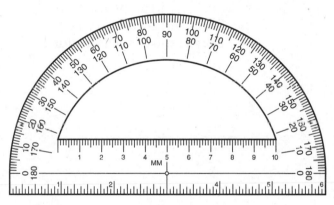

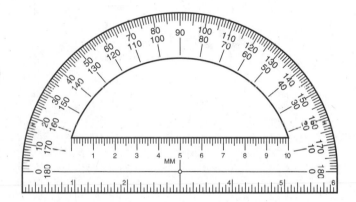

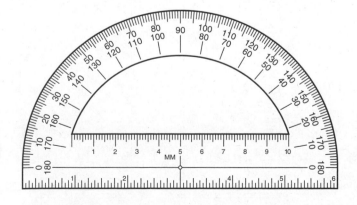

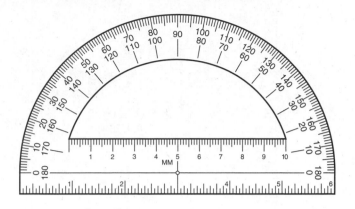

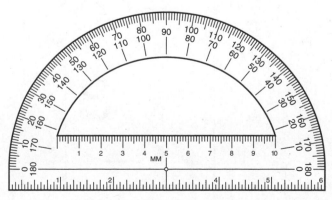

Rulers

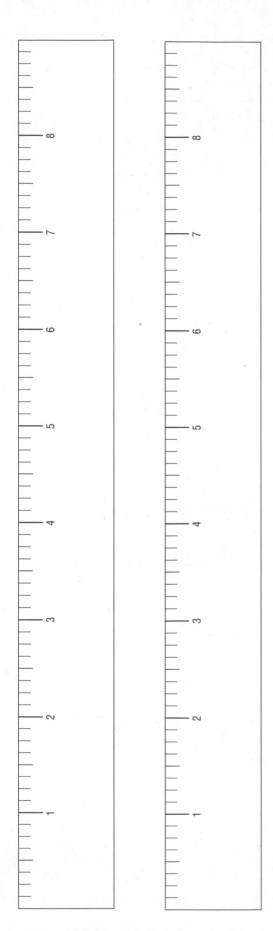

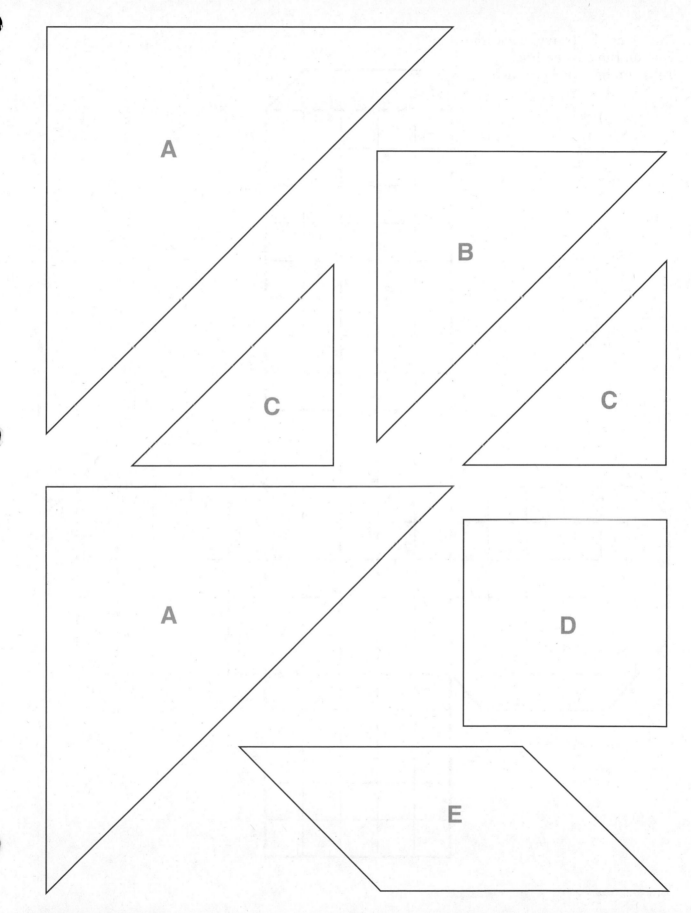

Cube Pattern

Cut along the heavy black lines.
Fold on the dashed lines.
Tabs can be taped or glued.

Cylinder Pattern

Cut along the heavy black lines.
Fold on the dashed lines.
Tabs can be taped or glued.

Cut along the heavy black lines.
Fold on the dashed lines.
Tabs can be taped or glued.

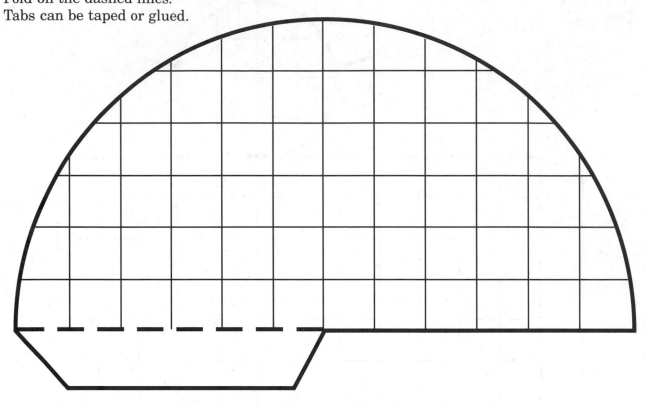

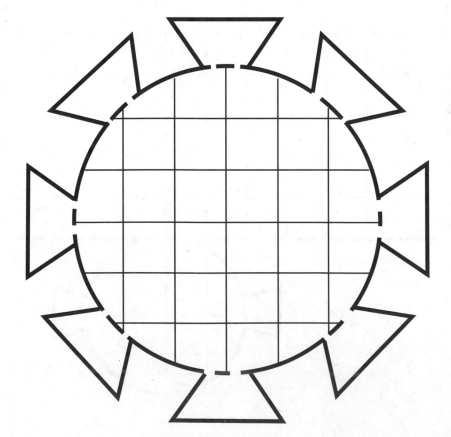

Pyramid Pattern

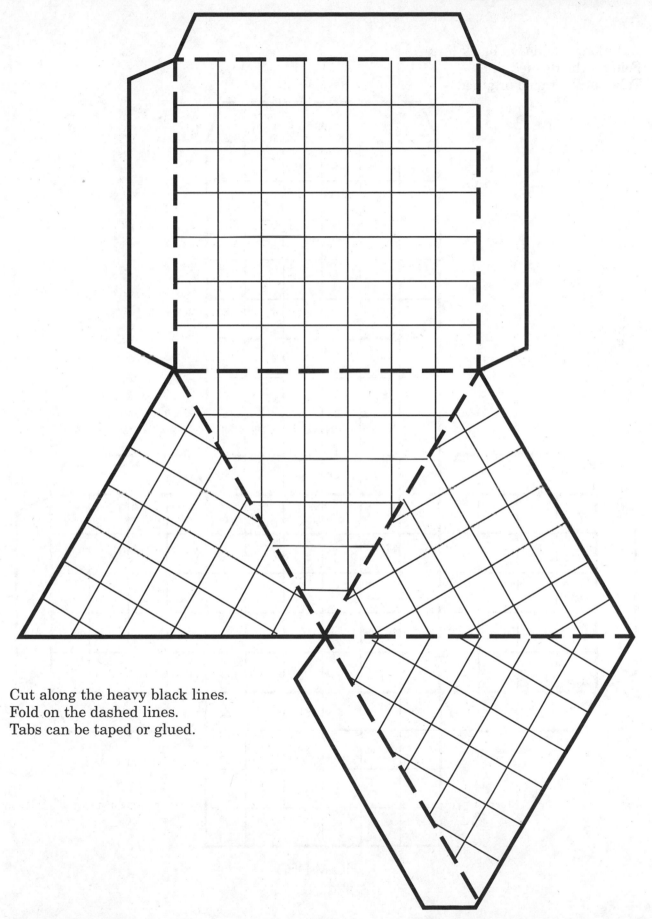

Cut along the heavy black lines.
Fold on the dashed lines.
Tabs can be taped or glued.

Rectangular Prism Pattern

Cut along the heavy black lines.
Fold on the dashed lines.
Tabs can be taped or glued.

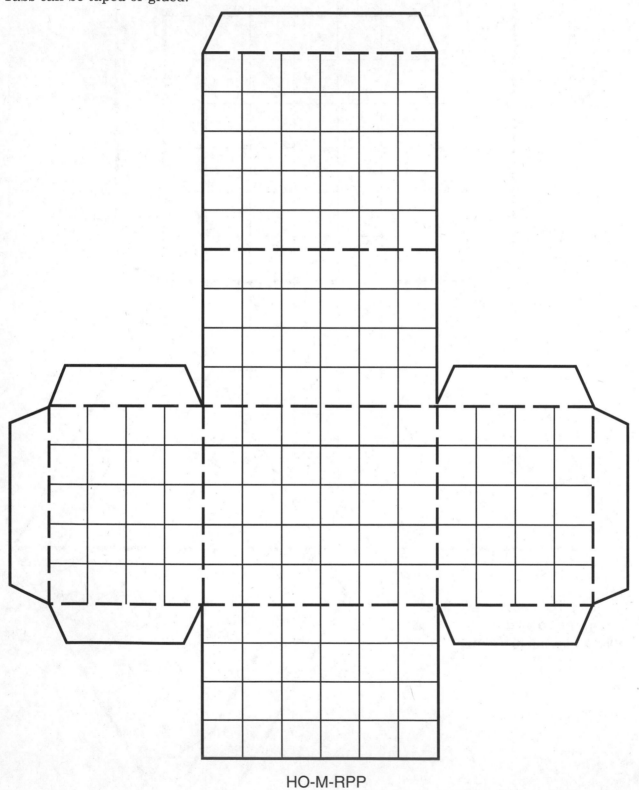

HO-M-RPP

The Tools of Algebra
Teaching Notes and Overview

 ## *Mini-Project*
Multiple Equations
(p. 31 of this booklet)

Use With Lesson 1-5.

Objective Use manipulatives to identify and solve open sentences.

Materials
beans, counters, or other small objects

This activity requires students to work in groups of four to find ways to represent solutions of sets of equations using symbols.

Sample Answers

1. ☼ = 1, ✧ = 3, ☐ = 4
2. ☼ = 8, ✧ = 5, ☐ = 2
3. ☼ = 5, ✧ = 3, ☐ = 4
4. ☼ = 8, ✧ = 4, ☐ = 10
5. ☼ = 4, ✧ = 7, ☐ = 2
6. ☼ = 12, ✧ = 9, ☐ = 3

 ## *Using Overhead Manipulatives*
Gathering Data
(p. 32 of this booklet)

Use With Lesson 1-7.

Objective Gather and record data.

Materials
transparency pens*
blank transparencies
* = available in Overhead Manipulative Resources Kit

- Students are asked to think about how data is collected and the types of data that should be collected.
- Extension questions ask students to conduct a survey and analyze the results.

Answers
Answers appear on the teacher demonstration instructions on page 32.

 ## *Algebra Activity Recording Sheet*
Scatter Plots
(p. 33 of this booklet)

Use With Lesson 1-7 as a preview activity. This corresponds to the activity on page 39 in the Student Edition.

Objective Construct and interpret scatter plots.

Materials
centimeter ruler

An expanded table like the one shown in the Student Edition has been provided so that students may record data for the entire class.

You might ask students to predict the relationship before beginning the activity.

Answers
See Teacher Wraparound Edition p. 39.

 ## *Using Overhead Manipulatives*
Scatter Plots
(p. 34 of this booklet)

Use With Lesson 1-7.

Objective Graph number pairs on a coordinate system to determine if there is a relationship.

Materials
cloth tape measures
blank transparency
coordinate grid transparency*
transparency pen*
projectable graphing calculator, if available
* = available in Overhead Manipulative Resources Kit

You will find the ordered pair (circumference, height) for each student as they practice naming ordered pairs. You will create a scatter plot of this data and look for relationships between data. Use the overhead graphing calculator if possible to input data and produce a scatter plot.

Answers
Answers appear on the teacher demonstration instructions on page 34.

![people icon] **Mini-Project**
(Use with Lesson 1-5)

Multiple Equations

Work in groups. Assign each person in the group a number from 1 to 4. Use the large shapes below to assign a value to each shape in each set of equations. Work together to place counters in each shape in order to make each set of equations true. Each group member is responsible for making his or her numbered equation in the set true.

	Equation 1	Equation 2	Equation 3	Equation 4
1.	$\circledast + \diamond = 4$	$\square = 4$	$\square - \circledast = 3$	$\diamond + \diamond = 6$
2.	$\diamond + 1 = 6$	$\square + \diamond = 7$	$\circledast - \diamond = 3$	$\circledast - \square = 6$
3.	$2\circledast = 10$	$\circledast - \diamond = 2$	$3\diamond = 9$	$\circledast - \square = 1$
4.	$\dfrac{\square}{2} = 5$	$\square + \circledast = 18$	$\circledast \div 2 = \diamond$	$\circledast \times \diamond = 32$
5.	$4\circledast - \diamond = 9$	$\circledast + \diamond = 11$	$8\square = 4\circledast$	$\circledast + \diamond + \square = 13$
6.	$2\diamond \div \square = 6$	$6\circledast = 8\diamond$	$2\circledast = 7\square + 3$	$4\square - 10 = 2$

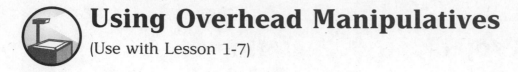

Using Overhead Manipulatives

(Use with Lesson 1-7)

Gathering Data

Objective Gather and record data.

Materials
- transparency pen*
- blank transparencies

* = available in Overhead Manipulative Resources Kit

Demonstration
Collecting Data

- Tell students "Suppose our class has been hired to develop an ad campaign to convince the students in our school to buy a new magazine. Our first step is to learn about the students in our school. The pieces of information you will gather are called **data**. Then you will analyze the data." Write the following questions on a transparency.

  1. How many people should we survey and how should we choose the sample?

  2. What questions should we ask?

  3. How should we gather the data? **Answers will vary.**

- Ask students to consider the first question. Record all reasonable ideas and help them to choose the best one to use. **Answers will vary.**

- Ask students to consider the second question. On a blank transparency, record all reasonable questions. Then go back over the list and help students eliminate questions that will not help them learn about the students in the school. **Answers will vary.**

- Have students generate ideas about how to gather the data. **Sample answers include distributing printed questionnaires and having someone ask individuals the questions and record their answers.**

Extension
Conducting a Survey

- Have students work in small groups to conduct a survey of the cars in a parking lot. They should determine what characteristics they will study and record their data and analyses on transparencies. Ask each group to share and discuss their survey with the class. Then ask of what use the information might be. **Sample answers: We found that many cars needed to be washed, so we might use the information to start a car-washing service. We found that many of the cars were either blue or silver; if we wanted to sell license plate holders, we should choose colors that look good with blue and silver.**

Algebra Activity Recording Sheet

(Use with the activity on page 39 in Lesson 1-7 Preview of Student Edition.)

Scatter Plots

Materials: centimeter ruler

Collect the Data

• Work with a partner. Use a centimeter ruler to measure the length of your partner's height and arm span to the nearest centimeter. Record the data in the table below.

Name	Height (cm)	Arm Span (cm)

• Make a list of ordered pairs in which the *x*-coordinate represents height and the *y*-coordinate represents arm span.

• Use the coordinate grid at the right to graph the ordered pairs (height, arm span).

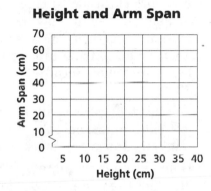

Height and Arm Span

Analyze the Data

1. Does there appear to be a trend in the data? If so, describe the trend.

Make a Conjecture

2. Estimate the arm span of a person whose height is 60 inches.

3. How does a person's arm span compare to his or her height?

4. Suppose the variable *x* represents height, and the variable *y* represents arm span. Write an expression for arm span.

Extend the Activity

5. Collect and graph data to determine whether a relationship exists between height and shoe length. Explain your results on the back of this paper.

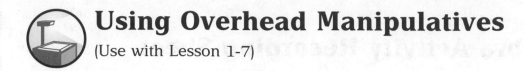

Using Overhead Manipulatives

(Use with Lesson 1-7)

Scatter Plots

Objective Graph number pairs on a coordinate system to determine if there is a relationship.

Materials
- transparency pen*
- coordinate grid transparency*
- cloth tape measures
- projectable graphing calculator, if available
- blank transparency

* = available in Overhead Manipulative Resources Kit

Demonstration
Constructing a Scatter Plot

- Attach a cloth measuring tape to a wall so that it can be used for measuring height. Have a student stand against the wall. Measure the student's height in inches and record on a blank transparency. Use another measuring tape to measure the circumference of the student's head in inches. Record this measure. **Sample answers: 58 inches; 20 inches**

- Tell students, "You can organize this data using the ordered pair (circumference, height)." Ask them to name the ordered pair for this student. **Sample answer: (20, 58)**

- Display the coordinate grid transparency. Review plotting ordered pairs and plot the sample ordered pair on the grid, with circumference on the horizontal axis and height on the vertical axis.

- Find the ordered pair for each student and plot the data on the coordinate grid transparency. Have students graph the data at their seats.

- Point out that the graph you have made is called a **scatter plot**, and that scatter plots can be used to look for relationships between data.

- Ask students whether there appears to be a relationship between head circumference and height. **Height is about 3 times head circumference.**

Extension
Using a Graphing Calculator

Use computer graphing software and a PC Viewer, or a graphing calculator and ViewScreen to plot points for a scatter plot of neck circumference and height. Use data from at least 10 students. Ask students whether there appears to be a relationship between neck circumference and height. Ask students to explain their findings. **There will probably be less relationship between neck circumference and height than there was between head circumference and height; Neck circumference can be affected by musculature and weight.**

2 Integers
Teaching Notes and Overview

 Mini-Project
Negative Numbers in History
(p. 37 of this booklet)

Use With Lesson 2-1.

Objective To research the history of negative numbers.

Materials
reference books or internet

Students work in groups to research the history of negative numbers and present their findings to the class.

Sample Answers

1. A bad image; Europeans refused to accept negative numbers. Descartes said a negative solution of a problem was false.

2. In the Renaissance, explorers in all fields became more creative, and new discoveries expanded the practical requirements of mathematics.

3. Money problems involving debts and credits, temperature problems, measurements above and below sea level, weight gains and losses, football gains and losses of yards, card games with negative scores.

4. It comes from the practice of writing losses in company accounting records in red ink. It started in the Renaissance period, before the use of a minus sign, to indicate a negative number.

5. 47 B.C.; No, there is no zero year, so A.D. 1 comes immediately after 1 B.C.

6. To express time before the hour such as "15 minutes before 3 o'clock."

 Using Overhead Manipulatives
Adding Integers
(pp. 38–39 of this booklet)

Use With Lesson 2-2.

Objective Use 1-tiles to model addition of integers.

Materials
transparency pen*
integer mat transparency*
1-tiles*
* = available in Overhead Manipulative Resources Kit

This demonstration contains two activities.

• Demonstration 1 shows how to model the addition of integers having the same signs.

• Demonstration 2 shows how to model the addition of integers when the signs are different.

• Extension questions ask students to model and solve integer addition problems independently.

Answers
Answers appear on the teacher demonstration instructions on pages 38–39.

 Algebra Activity Recording Sheet
Adding Integers
(p. 40 of this booklet)

Use With Lesson 2-2 as a preview activity. This corresponds to the activity on pages 62–63 in the Student Edition.

Objective Use 1-tiles to model addition of integers.

Materials
1-tiles*
integer mat

Integer mats are provided so that students have space to draw their own models of integer addition problems.

Answers
See Teacher Wraparound Edition pp. 62–63.

Using Overhead Manipulatives

Subtracting Integers
(p. 41 of this booklet)

Use With Lesson 2-3.

Objective Use 1-tiles to model subtraction of integers.

Materials
1-tiles*
integer mat transparency*
* = available in Overhead Manipulative Resources Kit

This demonstration contains two activities.

• Demonstration 1 shows how to model the subtraction of integers having the same signs.

• Demonstration 2 shows how to model the subtraction of integers when the signs are different.

Answers
Answers appear on the teacher demonstration instructions on page 41.

Using Overhead Manipulatives

Multiplying Integers
(pp. 42–43 of this booklet)

Use With Lesson 2-4.

Objective Use 1-tiles to model multiplication of integers.

Materials
1-tiles*
integer mat transparency*
transparency pen*
* = available in Overhead Manipulative Resources Kit

This demonstration contains two activities.

• Demonstration 1 shows how to model the multiplication of two positive integers or a positive and a negative integer.

• Demonstration 2 shows how to model the multiplication of two negative integers.

• Extension questions ask students to model and solve integer multiplication problems independently.

Answers
Answers appear on the teacher demonstration instructions on pages 42–43.

Mini-Project
(Use with Lesson 2-1)

Negative Numbers in History

Work in groups. Research the history of negative numbers. Find answers for the following exercises. Share the results of your group's study with the entire class.

1. Before the 16th century in Europe, what was the "image" of negative numbers? Find some examples in history to support your answer.

2. What happened around the 16th century that caused people to need to use negative numbers?

After your research is completed, answer the following questions.

3. What kind of practical problems have you met that required the use of negative numbers?

4. A company is said to be operating "in the red" if it is spending more money than it is making. Find out where the expression "in the red" came from.

5. A man died in A.D. 5 at the age of 51 years. In what year was he born? Can you use the rules for adding and subtracting integers to solve this problem? Explain.

6. In telling time, how is the idea of a negative number often used?

Chapter 2

Using Overhead Manipulatives

(Use with Lesson 2-2)

Adding Integers

> **Objective** Use 1-tiles to model addition of integers.
>
> **Materials**
> - transparency pen*
> - 1-tiles*
> - integer mat transparency*
>
> * = available in Overhead Manipulative Resources Kit

Demonstration for Activity One
Adding Integers with the Same Signs

- Tell students that you can use 1-tiles to model operations with integers. There are positive 1-tiles and negative 1-tiles.

- Place a group of 3 negative 1-tiles on the mat. Then place a group of 5 negative 1-tiles on the mat. Tell students that each 1-tile represents -1. Ask students to state the addition sentence you have modeled.
  $-3 + (-5) = -8$

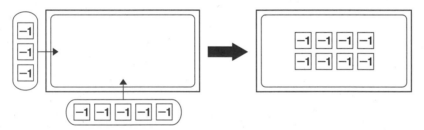

Demonstration for Activity Two
Adding Integers with Different Signs

- Clear the mat. Ask students how to show -3 on the mat. Place 3 negative 1-tiles on the mat. Ask students to show $+5$. Place 5 positive 1-tiles on the mat and write $-3 + 5 = ?$ at the base of the mat.
  3 negative 1-tiles; 5 positive 1-tiles

- Tell students "When you pair a positive 1-tile with a negative 1-tile, the result is zero. The pair of 1-tiles is called a **zero pair**." Tell them, "You can add or remove zero pairs without changing the value of the set."

- Remove all zero pairs from the mat. Then ask what remains on the mat.
  2 positive 1-tiles

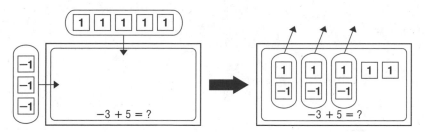

- Ask, "What is the sum of −3 and +5?" Have students complete the addition sentence on the mat. **2; −3 + 5 = 2**

Extension
Modeling Practice

Have students tell how to model the following sums. Have them draw each step at their seats as you model it on the mat.

a. −6 + 2 **Place 6 negative 1-tiles and 2 positive 1-tiles on the mat. Remove two zero pairs. The sum is −4.**

b. +6 + (−2) **Place 6 positive 1-tiles and 2 negative 1-tiles on the mat. Remove two zero pairs. The sum is 4.**

c. +8 + (−7) **Place 8 positive 1-tiles and 7 negative 1-tiles on the mat. Remove 7 zero pairs. The sum is 1.**

d. −8 + 7 **Place 8 negative 1-tiles and 7 positive 1-tiles on the mat. Remove 7 zero pairs. The sum is −1.**

Chapter 2

Algebra Activity Recording Sheet

(Use with the activity on pages 62–63 in Lesson 2-2 Preview of the Student Edition)

Adding Integers

Materials: integer mat, 1-tiles

Model
Use algebra tiles to model and find each sum.

1. $-2 + (-4)$

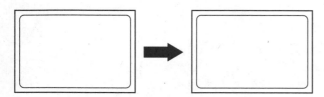

2. $-3 + (-5)$

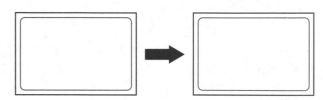

3. $-6 + (-1)$

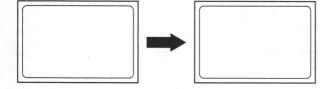

4. $-4 + (-5)$

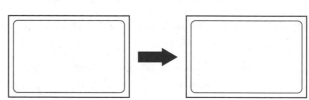

5. $-4 + 2$

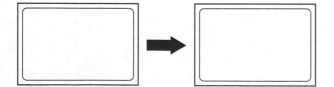

6. $2 + (-5)$

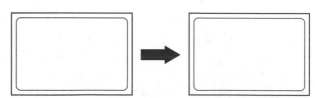

7. $-1 + 6$

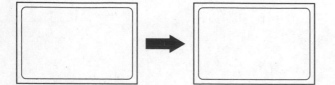

8. $4 + (-4)$

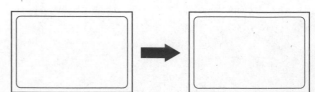

Using Overhead Manipulatives

(Use with Lesson 2-3)

Subtracting Integers

Objective Use 1-tiles to model subtraction of integers.

Materials
- 1-tiles*
- integer mat transparency*

* = available in Overhead Manipulative Resources Kit

Demonstration 1
Subtracting Integers with the Same Signs

- Place 7 positive 1-tiles on the mat and then remove 4 of them. Ask students what operation this suggests. Ask them to state an equation for this model. **Subtraction; 7 − 4 = 3**

- Clear the mat. Place 7 negative 1-tiles on the mat and then remove 4 of them. Ask students to state an equation for this model. **−7 − (−4) = −3**

Demonstration 2
Subtracting Integers with Different Signs

- Clear the mat. Tell students you want to model 7 − (−4). Ask them what you should start with to model 7. **7 positive 1-tiles**

- Tell students that since there are no negative 1-tiles on the mat, you cannot remove 4 negative 1-tiles. Remind them that placing a zero pair on the mat will not change the value. Place 4 zero pairs on the mat. Ask students what the value of the mat is. Remove 4 negative 1-tiles. Ask students to state an equation for this model. **7; 7 − (−4) = 11**

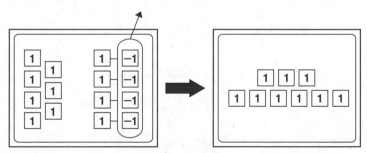

- To prepare students for independent practice, model the subtraction sentence −2 − (−5) = 3 as follows. Place 2 negative 1-tiles on the mat. Then place 3 zero pairs on the mat so there will be 5 negative 1-tiles to remove. Remove the 5 negative 1-tiles. The result is 3. Ask students how many zero pairs should be placed on the mat to model −4 − (−5). **1 zero pair**

Using Overhead Manipulatives

(Use with Lesson 2-4)

Multiplying Integers

Objective Use 1-tiles to model multiplication of integers.

Materials
- transparency pen*
- 1-tiles*
- integer mat transparency*

* = available in Overhead Manipulative Resources Kit

Demonstration 1
Multiplying Integers

- Remind students that 2×3 means *two sets of three items*. Tell them that modeling 2×3 means to place 2 sets of 3 positive 1-tiles on the mat. Model 2×3 using 1-tiles as shown. Ask students to complete the sentence $2 \times 3 = ?$ **6**

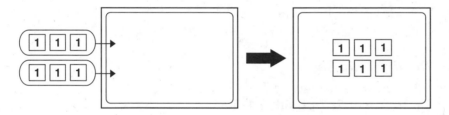

- Clear the mat. Place 2 sets of 3 negative 1-tiles on the mat. Ask students to state the multiplication sentence that has been modeled. $2 \times (-3) = -6$

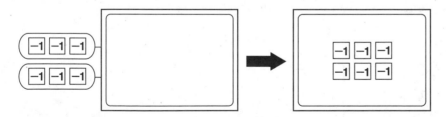

Demonstration 2
Multiplying Two Negative Integers

- Clear the mat. Tell students that since -2 is the opposite of 2, -2×3 means to *remove* 2 sets of 3 positive 1-tiles. Place 6 zero pairs on the mat. Then remove 2 sets of 3 positive 1-tiles. Ask students what the result is. Ask students to complete the multiplication sentence $-2 \times 3 = ?$ **6 negative 1-tiles or -6; -6**

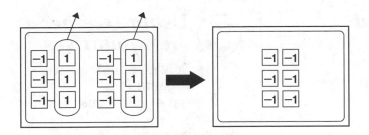

- Clear the mat. Write $-2 \times (-3)$ at the base of the mat. Ask students what this means. Ask them to describe how to model this problem. Have them draw each step as you model it. Ask students to complete the sentence $-2 \times (-3) = ?$ **Remove 2 sets of 3 negative 1-tiles; Place 6 zero pairs on the mat so that you can make 2 sets of 3 negative 1-tiles. There are 6 positive 1-tiles remaining. So, $-2 \times (-3) = +6$; 6**

Extension
Modeling Practice
Have students describe how to model the following products. Have them draw each step at their seats as you model it on the mat.

a. 3×5 **Place 3 sets of 5 positive 1-tiles on the mat. The product is 15.**

b. $3 \times (-5)$ **Place 3 sets of 5 negative 1-tiles on the mat. The product is −15.**

c. -3×5 **Place 15 zero pairs on the mat so you can make 3 groups of 5 positive 1-tiles. Remove 3 groups of 5 positive 1-tiles. 15 negative 1-tiles remain. The product is −15.**

d. $-3 \times (-5)$ **Place 15 zero pairs on the mat so you can make 3 groups of 5 negative 1-tiles. 15 positive 1-tiles remain. The product is 15.**

Ask students how they determined the number of zero pairs to use when multiplying by a negative number. **Find the product of the absolute value of the factors.**

3 Equations
Teaching Notes and Overview

 Using Overhead Manipulatives

Distributive Property
(pp. 47–48 of this booklet)

Use With Lesson 3-1.

Objective Visualize the distributive property by modeling a geometric interpretation.

Materials
algebra tiles*
blank transparency
transparency pen*
* = available in Overhead Manipulative Resources Kit

- This demonstration models the Distributive Property by finding the area of algebra tiles. Students practice using algebra tiles to make rectangles with various areas.
- The extension activity provides more practice with modeling areas using rectangles.

Answers
Answers appear on the teacher demonstration instructions on pages 47–48.

 Using Overhead Manipulatives

Solving Equations with Algebra Tiles
(pp. 49–50 of this booklet)

Use With Lesson 3-3.

Objective Use 1-tiles and x-tiles to solve equations.

Materials
1-tiles*
x-tiles*
equation mat transparency*
transparency pen*
* = available in Overhead Manipulative Resources Kit

This demonstration contains three activities.
- Demonstration 1 models how to solve addition equations using algebra tiles.
- Demonstration 2 models how to solve subtraction equations using algebra tiles.
- The extension activity provides more modeling practice for students to try independently.

Answers
Answers appear on the teacher demonstration instructions on pages 49–50.

Algebra Activity Recording Sheet

Solving Equations Using Algebra Tiles
(p. 51 of this booklet)

Use With Lesson 3-3 and 3-4 as a preview activity. This corresponds to the activity on pages 108–109 in the Student Edition.

Objective Use algebra tiles to model and solve equations.

Materials
algebra tiles
equation mat

Answers
See Teacher Wraparound Edition pp. 108–109.

Using Overhead Manipulatives

Two-Step Equations
(pp. 52–53 of this booklet)

Use With Lesson 3-5.

Objective Use 1-tiles and x-tiles to model and solve two-step equations.

Materials
1-tiles*
x-tiles*
equation mat transparency*
transparency pen*
blank transparency
* = available in Overhead Manipulative Resources Kit

- This demonstration shows how to use algebra tiles to model and solve two-step equations.
- The extension activity shows students how to use paper-and-pencil models to solve equations when algebra tiles are not available.

Answers
Answers appear on the teacher demonstration instructions on pages 52–53.

Mini-Project

Exploring Two-Step Equations
(p. 54 of this booklet)

Use With Lesson 3-5.

Objective Practice modeling and solving two-step equations.

Materials
rectangular eraser
wooden ruler
rolls of pennies, nickels, dimes, and quarters

Students work in pairs to model two-step equations and their solutions using a balance they create from an eraser and a ruler.

Answers

1. Since 2 rolls of nickels and 1 roll of dimes weigh the same as 5 rolls of dimes, then 2 rolls of nickels weigh the same as 4 rolls of dimes. Thus, 2 rolls of dimes weigh the same as one roll of nickels.

2. Yes

3. 2

4. 2 dimes

5. Yes; 2 pennies from each side

6. 4

7. 2 pennies

8. Subtraction

9. Division

10. Yes

11. No

12. Yes

13. Yes

Chapter 3

Algebra Activity

Discovering Patterns in Mathematics
(p. 55 of this booklet)

Use With Lesson 3-6.

Objective Explore relationships between perimeter and area using tables and algebra tiles.

Materials
graph paper or algebra tiles*
* = available in Overhead Manipulative Resources Kit

Students use either graph paper or algebra tiles to construct figures with various perimeters and areas. They use tables to look for patterns in the relationships between perimeter and area.

Answers

Table: 4, 6, 8, 10, 12, 14, 16, 18, 20, 22

1. The greatest possible perimeter is 2 more than twice the area.

2. $2x + 2$

Tables: 8, 10, 12, 14, 16; 8, 10, 12, 14, 16

3. When A is even, $P = A + 4$; when A is odd, $P = A + 5$.

4a. $(x + 4)$ sq. units

4b. $(x + 5)$ sq. units

Using Overhead Manipulatives

(Use with Lesson 3-1)

Distributive Property

> **Objective** Visualize the Distributive Property by modeling a geometric interpretation.
>
> **Materials**
> - algebra tiles*
> - transparency pen*
> - blank transparency
>
> * = available in Overhead Manipulative Resources Kit

Demonstration
Finding Areas of Algebra Tiles

- Remind students that the area of a rectangle is the product of its length and width. Place a 1×1 tile and a $1 \times x$ tile at the top of a blank transparency. Label the sides as shown below. Ask students to state the area of each tile. Tell students they will use the algebra tiles to check the Distributive Property. **1 square unit, *x* square units**

- Model a rectangle with a width of 1 unit and a length of $x + 2$ units as shown. Ask students to find the area of the rectangle. **x + 2 square units**

- Have students use tiles to make rectangles with the following areas. **Sample answers shown.**

$3x + 1$

$x + 1$ $3x$

$3x + 3$

(continued on the next page)

- Write $3(x + 1) = 3x + 1$ on the transparency. Tell students that algebra tiles can be used to check whether the equation is true. Show them $3(x + 1)$ means

Have students compare this with the rectangle they made for $3x + 1$ earlier. Ask whether the areas are the same. Ask students if the equation is true and why. Ask students if they made a rectangle that has the same area as $3(x + 1)$. **No; no, since the areas are not the same, $3(x + 1)$ is not equal to $3x + 1$; yes, $3x + 3$.**

Extension
More Modeling Practice
Ask students how to use tiles to show $2 + 4$ (see drawing at the right). Place a $1 \times x$ tile below each 1×1 tile as shown. Then ask whether this shows $x(2 + 4)$.
No, it shows $(x + 1)(2 + 4)$.

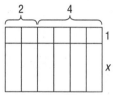

48

Using Overhead Manipulatives
(Use with Lesson 3-3)

Solving Equations with Algebra Tiles

Objective Use algebra tiles to solve equations.

Materials
- algebra tiles*
- transparency pen*
- equation mat transparency*

* = available in Overhead Manipulative Resources Kit

Demonstration 1
Solving Addition Equations

- Place an *x*-tile and 3 positive 1-tiles on the left side of the equation mat transparency. Remind students that the *x*-tile represents an unknown value, *x*. Ask them what sum is shown on the left side of the mat. Place 7 positive 1-tiles on the right side of the mat. Ask students what number is represented on the right side of the mat. **x + 3; 7**

- Tell students that the mat is a model of the equation $x + 3 = 7$. Write the equation at the base of the mat.

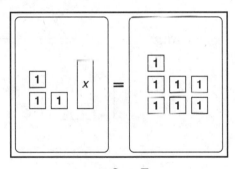

$$x + 3 = 7$$

- Tell students, "If you remove three matching 1-tiles from each side of the mat, you can see how many 1-tiles must be equal to an *x*-tile in order to make the equation true." Ask, "What must the value of *x* be for this equation to be true?" **4**

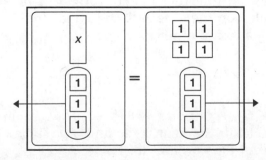

- Say, "You can check this solution by substituting it in the original equation. Since 4 + 3 = 7, our solution is correct."

Chapter 3

Demonstration 2
Solving Subtraction Equations

- Clear the mat. Place 7 positive 1-tiles on the left side of the mat and an x-tile and 3 negative 1-tiles on the right side of the mat. Ask students what equation is represented. Write the equation at the base of the mat.
7 = x − 3

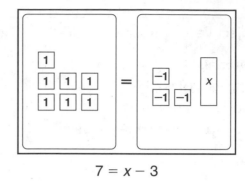

$$7 = x - 3$$

- Remind students that you can find the value of x by removing matching 1-tiles on the left and right sides. Point out that in this case there are no matching 1-tiles. Add 3 positive 1-tiles to each side. Point out that there are now 3 zero pairs on the right side.

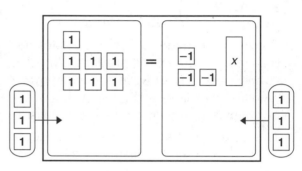

- Remove the zero pairs. Ask what the remaining tiles show. **10 = x**

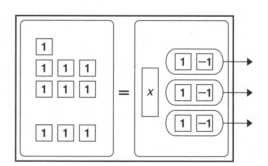

- Ask students how to check the solution. **Substitute 10 for *x* in the original equation. Since 7 = 10 − 3, the solution is correct.**

- Ask students how you determined what unit tiles to add. **You add 1-tiles to make zero pairs with all the 1-tiles on the side with the *x*-tile, and the same number and kind of 1-tiles to the other side.**

Extension
More Modeling Practice

Ask students how to model and solve the equation $x + 3 = -7$. Have them draw each step at their seats and model it. **Place an *x*-tile and 3 positive 1-tiles on the left side and 7 negative 1-tiles on the right side. Add 3 negative 1-tiles to each side and remove the zero pairs on the left side. The *x*-tile must equal 10 negative 1-tiles.**

50

Algebra Activity Recording Sheet

(Use with the Lesson 3-3 and 3-4 Preview activity on pages 108–109 in the Student Edition.)

Solving Equations Using Algebra Tiles

Materials: algebra tiles, equation mat

Use algebra tiles to model and solve each equation.

1. $3 + x = 7$

2. $x + 4 = 5$

3. $6 = x + 4$

4. $5 = 1 + x$

5. $x + 2 = -2$

6. $x - 3 = 2$

7. $0 = x + 3$

8. $-2 = x + 1$

9. $3x = 3$

10. $2x = -8$

11. $6 = 3x$

12. $-4 = 2x$

Chapter 3

Using Overhead Manipulatives

(Use with Lesson 3-5)

Two-Step Equations

Objective Use algebra tiles to model and solve two-step equations.

Materials
- algebra tiles*
- transparency pen*
- blank transparency
- equation mat transparency*

* = available in Overhead Manipulative Resources Kit

Demonstration
Modeling Two-Step Equations

- Remind students that you can use algebra tiles to model equations and that an x-tile represents an unknown amount. Place 3 x-tiles and 4 positive 1-tiles on the left side of the mat. Ask students what sum is modeled. Place 16 positive 1-tiles on the right side. Ask what equation is modeled. Write the equation at the base of the mat transparency. **$3x + 4$; $3x + 4 = 16$**

- Remind students that the two sides of the mat represent equal quantities. Ask students whether you can remove an equal number of 1-tiles from each side without changing the value of the equation. **Yes, you can remove 4 positive 1-tiles from each side of the mat.**

- Remove 4 positive 1-tiles from each side. Ask students why you removed 4 unit tiles from each side. **To get the x-tiles by themselves on one side.**

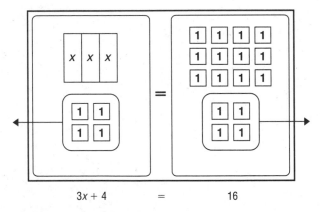

- Ask students to state the equation now shown. Write the equation at the base of the mat below the original equation. Separate the remaining 1-tiles into 3 equal groups to correspond to the 3 x-tiles. Tell students they must match an equal number of 1-tiles to each x-tile. **$3x = 12$**

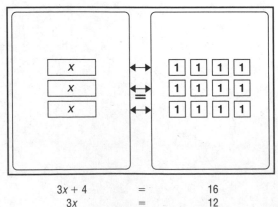

(continued on the next page)

- Ask students how many 1-tiles each x-tile must equal. Ask, "What is the value of x in this equation?" **4 positive 1-tiles; $x = 4$**

- Show students how to check the solution by setting up the original equation and then replacing each x-tile with 4 1-tiles. Ask, "Is the equation still true?" **yes**

- Clear the mat. Review the meaning of zero pairs. Ask students what happens to an equation if a zero pair is added to or subtracted from a side. Write the equation $3x - 3 = 15$ at the top of the mat and ask students to describe how to model this equation. Model the equation. **An equivalent equation results; Place 3 x-tiles and 3 negative 1-tiles on the left side of the mat. Place 15 positive 1-tiles on the right side.**

- Add 3 positive 1-tiles to each side. Ask whether the value of the equation has changed. **no**

- Point out the 3 zero pairs on the left side of the equation. Remove the zero pairs. Ask students to state the equation now shown. Record the equation at the base of the mat. **$3x = 18$**

$$3x - 3 = 15$$

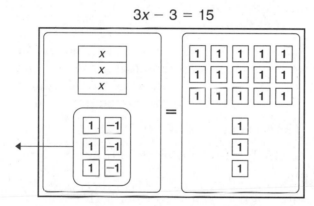

- Separate the remaining 1-tiles into 3 equal groups to correspond to the 3 x-tiles. Ask students how many 1-tiles correspond to each x-tile. Ask, "What is the value of x in this equation?" **6 positive 1-tiles; $x = 6$**

Extension

Show students how they can use paper-and-pencil models to solve equations if algebra tiles are not available. On a blank transparency, draw two boxes with an equals sign between them. In the box on the left, draw 2 x's and 4 circles with positive signs. In the box on the right, draw 2 circles with negative signs. Ask students what equation you have modeled. Add 4 zero pairs to the right side. Then indicate removing 4 positive 1-tiles from each side by circling them and drawing arrows out of the boxes. Draw a ring around 2 equal groups on the right side to find the value of x. **$2x + 4 = -2$; $x = -3$**

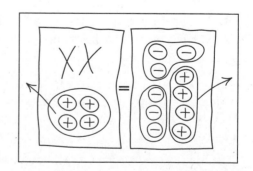

Mini-Project

(Use with Lesson 3-5)

Exploring Two-Step Equations

Materials: rectangular eraser, wooden ruler, rolls of pennies, nickels, dimes, and quarters

Work in pairs to solve the following problems.

Marguerite is a bank teller. When a customer brings in rolls of coins, Marguerite weighs them to make sure that they contain the correct number of coins. One day she noticed that 2 rolls of nickels and 1 roll of dimes weigh the same as 5 rolls of dimes.

1. Explain how you could determine the number of rolls of dimes that weigh the same as 1 roll of nickels.

Place a rectangular eraser on its edge on a flat surface. Place a wooden ruler across the eraser so that it balances, as shown at the right. Carefully stack 2 nickels and 1 dime on one end. Then stack 5 dimes on the other end.

2. If you remove one dime from each side, does the ruler remain balanced?

3. Now remove one of the nickels. Removing one at a time, how many dimes must be removed in order for the ruler to be balanced again?

4. How many dimes equal the weight of one nickel?

Stack 3 quarters and 2 pennies on the left end of the ruler and stack 8 pennies on the other end.

5. Can you remove an equal number of the same coin from both stacks and still keep the ruler balanced? What coins are they?

6. Remove two of the quarters. Removing one at a time, how many pennies must be removed in order for the ruler to be balanced again?

7. How many pennies equal the weight of one quarter?

8. What mathematical operation describes what you did in Exercises 2 and 5?

9. What mathematical operation describes what you did in Exercises 3 and 6?

Scales A and B at the right are balanced. The objects shown are the same weight in all the figures. Decide which of the scales in Exercises 10–13 are really balanced. Write yes or no.

10.
11.
12.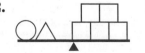
13.

Algebra Activity

(Use with Lesson 3-6)

Discovering Patterns in Mathematics

Materials: graph paper or algebra tiles

In mathematics, formulas are rules for working with numbers. Mathematicians have developed these rules by observing patterns in their work.

Use either graph paper or algebra tiles to construct figures with the greatest possible perimeter given the areas in the table below. Record your results in the table.

A	1	2	3	4	5	6	7	8	9	10
P										

Use the data in the table above to answer these questions.

1. What pattern can you find?

2. Using this pattern, what is the greatest perimeter for a figure with an area of x square units?

Using either graph paper or algebra tiles again, find the least possible perimeter. Draw figures with areas from 3 square units to 12 square units. Use the tables below to record your results.

A	3	5	7	9	11
P					

A	4	6	8	10	12
P					

Use the data in the tables to answer these questions.

3. Can you find a pattern? (*Hint*: Subtract each area from the corresponding perimeter.)

4. Predict the least possible perimeter for a figure with an area of x units, if

   a. x is even.   **b.** x is odd.

Chapter 3

4

Factors and Fractions
Teaching Notes and Overview

Mini-Project
Rules for Divisibility
(p. 58 of this booklet)

Use With Lesson 4-1.

Objective To work with additional divisibility rules.

Materials
none

Students work in small groups to determine and test divisibility rules for 4, 8, 9, 11, and 12.

Answers

1. yes

2. no

3. yes

4. yes

5. Since any multiple of 100 is divisible by 4, if the number formed by the tens digit is divisible by 4, then the entire number is divisible by 4.

6. A number is divisible by 8 if its last three digits are divisible by 8.

7. A number is divisible by 9 if the sum of its digits is divisible by 9.

8. A number is divisible by 12 if it is divisible by 3 and 4.

9. 2, 3, 6, 9

10. 2

11. 2, 3, 4, 6, 9, 11, 12

12. 2, 3, 4, 5, 6, 8, 9, 10, 11, 12

Using Overhead Manipulatives
Finding Factors
(p. 59 of this booklet)

Use With Lesson 4-1.

Objective Use rectangles to model factors.

Materials
overhead grid transparency*
transparency pens*
grid paper
* = available in Overhead Manipulative Resources Kit

- This demonstration shows students how rectangles can be drawn as models of factors for given whole numbers. Students describe the relationship between rectangular arrangements of squares and pairs of whole number factors of a number.

- The extension activity provides independent practice in modeling factors of whole numbers using rectangles.

Answers
Answers appear on the teacher demonstration instructions on page 59.

Algebra Activity Recording Sheet
Base 2
(p. 60 of this booklet)

Use With Lesson 4-2 as a follow-up activity. This corresponds to the activity on page 158 in the Student Edition.

Objective To become familiar with a base two system of numbers and convert between decimal and binary numbers.

Materials
none

Students practice converting decimal numbers into base two and binary numbers into base 10. The lesson extension introduces other bases such as 5 and 8 as well.

Answers
See Teacher Wraparound Edition p. 158.

Algebra Activity
Prime Numbers
(p. 61 of this booklet)

Use with Lesson 4-3.

Objective Use a calculator to work with formulas for finding prime numbers.

Materials
calculator

Students test formulas for finding prime numbers by making and analyzing tables of values.

Answers

1. 3, 7, 15, 31, 63, 127, 255, 511, 1023
2. 15, 63, 255, 511, 1023
3. 43, 47, 53, 61, 71, 83, 97, 113, 131
4. yes
5. 41

Using Overhead Manipulatives

Equivalent Fractions
(p. 62 of this booklet)

Use With Lesson 4-6.

Objective Use models to investigate fractions.

Materials
transparency pens*
blank transparency
inch ruler*
* = available in Overhead Manipulative Resources Kit

- Demonstration 1 uses a rectangle divided into equal parts to show that a fraction represents part of a whole.
- Demonstration 2 uses two identical rectangles divided up differently to show equivalent fractions.
- The extension activity asks students to draw their own model of equivalent fractions.

Answers
Answers appear on the teacher demonstration instructions on page 62.

Algebra Activity Recording Sheet

A Half-Life Simulation
(p. 63 of this booklet)

Use With Lesson 4-6 as a follow-up activity. This corresponds to the activity on page 180 in the Student Edition.

Objective Perform a simulation to learn about half-life.

Materials
50 pennies
shoe box

Answers
See Teacher Wraparound Edition p. 180.

Mini-Project

Operations with Scientific Notation
(p. 64 of this booklet)

Use With Lesson 4-8.

Objective To multiply and divide numbers written in scientific notation.

Materials
none

Students work in small groups and use the rules for products and quotients of powers to multiply or divide two numbers written in scientific notation.

Answers

1. 7.93×10^{14}
2. 2.51×10^{4}
3. 7.5×10^{12}
4. 7.37751×10^{-6}
5. about 1.86×10^{5} miles per second
6. about 5×10^{2} or 500 seconds

Chapter 4

Mini-Project

(Use with Lesson 4-1)

Rules for Divisibility

Work in small groups.

You have learned how to determine whether a number is divisible by 2, 3, 5, 6, or 10. There are also rules for divisibility by other whole numbers.

For example, a number is divisible by 4 if its last two digits form a number divisible by 4.

Use the test to determine whether each number is divisible by 4. Write yes or no.

  1. 42,172   **2.** 540,138   **3.** 4,937,728   **4.** 1,700,380

Is 4500 divisible by 4? Since zero is divisible by 4, any number that is a multiple of 100 will be divisible by 4.

  5. Use the information above to explain why the test for 4 works for any number.

  6. Verify that all multiples of 1000 are divisible by 8. Use this information to write a rule for divisibility by 8 that is similar to the rule for 4.

  7. Recall that a number is divisible by 3 if the sum of its digits is divisible by 3. Write a similar rule for divisibility by 9. Test it on several numbers.

  8. Recall that a number is divisible by 6 if it is divisible by 2 and 3. Write a similar rule for divisibility by 12.

The **alternating cross sum** of a number is formed as follows.

Example: 7 ☐3☐ 5 ☐6☐ 8 $7 + 5 + 8 = 20$ $3 + 6 = 9$

The alternating cross sum of 73,568 is $20 - 9 = 11$.

If the alternating cross sum of a number is divisible by 11, the number is divisible by 11.

Use the tests for divisibility to determine whether each number is divisible by 2, 3, 4, 5, 6, 8, 9, 10, 11, and 12.

  9. 16,002   **10.** 1742   **11.** 1188   **12.** 23,760

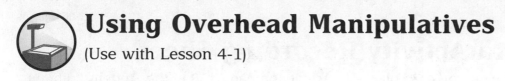

Using Overhead Manipulatives

(Use with Lesson 4-1)

Finding Factors

Objective Use rectangles to model factors.

Materials
- overhead grid transparency*
- transparency pens*
- grid paper
* = available in Overhead Manipulative Resources Kit

Demonstration
Modeling Factors

- Draw a 4 × 6 rectangle on the overhead grid transparency. Ask students how many squares are contained in the rectangle. **24**

- Tell them, "Here is a rectangular arrangement of 24 squares. There are other possible arrangements of 24 squares. Draw the remaining arrangements on your grid paper." **1 × 24, 2 × 12, 3 × 8, 24 × 1, 12 × 2, 8 × 3, 6 × 4**

- Say, "You know that 4 × 6 = 24. List all of the pairs of whole numbers that have a product of 24. **1 × 24, 2 × 12, 3 × 8, 4 × 6**

- Compare the list of whole numbers to the lengths of the sides of the rectangles you drew. What do you notice? **They are the same.**

- Tell students that the numbers that make up these pairs are called *factors*.

- Ask students to describe the relationship between rectangular arrangements of squares and pairs of whole number factors of a number. **You can find the pairs of factors of a given number by using rectangular arrangements of that number of squares.**

- Ask, "Can you arrange 17 squares in a rectangle so that one side of the rectangle is 2 units long? 3 units long? Did you know whether or not it could be done before you tried?" **no; no; Sample answer: Yes, because the only factors of 17 are 1 and 17.**

Extension
More Modeling Practice

Use grid paper to draw the rectangular arrangements for each number given. Then list all the factors for each number.

1. 18
   1 × 18, 2 × 9, 3 × 6

2. 9
   1 × 9, 3 × 3

3. 11
   1 × 11

Algebra Activity Recording Sheet

(Use with the Lesson 4-2 Follow-Up Activity on page 158 in the Student Edition.)

Base 2

Materials: none

Exercises

1. Express 1011_2 as an equivalent number in base 10.

Express each base 10 number as an equivalent number in base 2.

2. 6   **3.** 9   **4.** 15   **5.** 21

Extend the Activity

6. The first five place values for base 5 are shown. Any digit from 0 to 4 can be used to write a base 5 number. Write 179 in base 5.

7. **OPEN ENDED**   Write 314 as an equivalent number in a base other than 2, 5, or 10.

8. **OPEN ENDED**   Choose a base 10 number and write it as an equivalent number in base 8.

Algebra Activity

(Use with Lesson 4-3)

Prime Numbers

Materials: calculator

Prime numbers are whole numbers greater than 1 that have exactly two factors, 1 and the number itself. There are several ways to find prime numbers. The formulas $P = 2^n - 1$ and $P = n^2 - n + 41$, where n is a whole number greater than 1, can be used to find many prime numbers. However, not every number found using these formulas is prime.

1. Use the formula $P = 2^n - 1$ and a calculator to complete the table below. On some calculators, you can use the following keys to compute $2^n - 1$.

   2 $\boxed{y^x}$ n $\boxed{-}$ 1 $\boxed{=}$

n	2	3	4	5	6	7	8	9	10
P									

2. Which of the values of P in the table are <u>not</u> prime numbers? (*Hint*: Test each value using the divisibility rules discussed in Lesson 4-1.)

3. Use the formula $P = n^2 - n + 41$ and a calculator to complete the table below. You can use the following keys to compute $n^2 - n + 41$.

   n $\boxed{x^2}$ $\boxed{-}$ n $\boxed{+}$ 41 $\boxed{=}$

n	2	3	4	5	6	7	8	9	10
P									

4. Are all of the values of P in the table prime numbers?

5. Use a calculator to find the first value of n for which the formula $P = n^2 - n + 41$ produces a composite value for P. (*Hint:* This value of P is divisible by 41.)

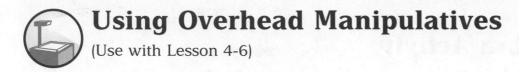

Using Overhead Manipulatives

(Use with Lesson 4-6)

Equivalent Fractions

Objective Use models to investigate fractions.

Materials
- inch ruler*
- transparency pens*
- blank transparency

* = available in Overhead Manipulative Resources Kit

Demonstration for Activity One
Representing Fractions

- Remind students that a fraction represents part of a whole. Use a ruler and the black transparency pen to draw a rectangle like the one shown. Tell students that it represents 1.

- Separate the rectangle into 12 equal parts. Use a colored transparency pen to shade one part. Ask students what fraction of the rectangle is shaded. $\frac{1}{12}$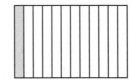

- Ask students how to represent $\frac{2}{12}$ on the same rectangle. **Shade 2 of the 12 parts.**

Demonstration for Activity Two
Equivalent Fractions

- Tell students that you are going to compare two fractions. Use a ruler and the black transparency pen to draw two identical rectangles.

- Separate the upper rectangle into 6 equal parts. Separate the bottom rectangle into 9 equal parts.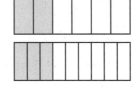

- Use a colored transparency pen to shade 2 parts of the upper rectangle. Then shade 3 parts of the lower rectangle. Ask students what fraction each shaded region represents. $\frac{2}{6}, \frac{3}{9}$

- Ask: Do these fractions represent the same number? How do you know? Are there other fractions that could name the same number? **Yes; the shaded regions are equal in size. Yes; Sample:** $\frac{4}{12}, \frac{5}{15}$

Extension
Modeling Equivalent Fractions
Draw a rectangle and separate it into 4 equal parts. Shade 3 parts. Ask students what fraction is represented. Ask students how you could change the drawing to show an equal fraction with a numerator of 8. Ask what fraction is represented. $\frac{3}{4}$, **Sample: Draw lines separating each of the 4 equal parts into 2 equal parts.;** $\frac{6}{8}$

Algebra Activity Recording Sheet

(Use with the Lesson 4-6 Follow-Up Activity on page 180 in the Student Edition.)

A Half-Life Simulation

Materials: 50 pennies, shoebox, grid paper

Collect the Data

Number of Half-Lives	1	2	3	4	5
Number of Pennies That Remain					

Analyze the Data

1.

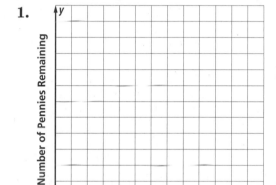

Number of Pennies Remaining

Number of Half-Lives

2. Describe the graph of the data.

Make a Conjecture

3. Use the expressions to predict how many pennies remain after three half-lives. Compare this number to the number in the table above. Explain any differences.

Mini-Project

(Use with Lesson 4-8)

Operations with Scientific Notation

You can use the rules for finding the product or quotient of powers to multiply or divide two numbers written in scientific notation.

Example

Multiply 3.918×10^{-4} by 4.15×10^8. Write the answer in scientific notation.

$(3.918 \times 10^{-4})(4.15 \times 10^8)$

$= (3.918 \times 4.15)(10^{-4} \times 10^8)$ *Associative and Commutative Properties of Multiplication*
$= (16.2597)(10^{-4+8})$ *Product of powers*
$= 16.2597 \times 10^4$ *Not scientific notation*
$= 1.62597 \times 10^1 \times 10^4$
$= 1.62597 \times 10^5$ *Scientific notation*

Work in small groups to solve the following problems. Write all answers in scientific notation.

1. Multiply $(6.1 \times 10^4)(1.3 \times 10^{10})$.

2. Divide $\dfrac{8.534 \times 10^6}{3.4 \times 10^2}$.

3. Divide $\dfrac{4.2 \times 10^8}{5.6 \times 10^{-5}}$.

4. Multiply $(8.17 \times 10^{-4})(9.03 \times 10^{-3})$.

5. Earth is 9.3×10^7 miles from the sun. Neptune is 2.8×10^9 miles from the sun. How many times farther from the sun is Neptune than Earth?

6. A light year is the distance light travels in one year. This distance is 5.8657×10^{12} miles. If the Andromeda Galaxy is 2.2×10^6 light years away from Earth, how many miles away from Earth is it?

7. Using the distance light travels in a year given in Exercise 6, find the speed of light in miles per second. Use 1 year = 365 days.

8. Using the information given in Exercise 5 and your answer to Exercise 7, determine how long, in seconds, it takes light to travel from the sun to Earth.

Rational Numbers
Teaching Notes and Overview

Algebra Activity
Fractions
(p. 69 of this booklet)

Use With Lesson 5-2 as a follow-up activity.

Objective Use a tangram to multiply and divide fractions and compute areas.

Materials
tangram
scissors

Students compute areas of pieces of a tangram, make comparisons, and multiply and divide fractions.

Answers

1. $\frac{1}{4}$ square unit

2. $\frac{1}{8}$ square unit

3. $\frac{1}{16}$ square unit

4. $\frac{1}{8}$ square unit; $\frac{1}{8}$ square unit

5a.

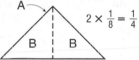

$2 \times \frac{1}{8} = \frac{1}{4}$

5b.

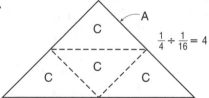

$\frac{1}{4} \div \frac{1}{16} = 4$

Algebra Activity Recording Sheet
Juniper Green
(p. 70 of this booklet)

Use With Lesson 5-6 as a follow-up activity. This corresponds to the activity on page 231 in the Student Edition.

Objective To play and analyze a game in which players find multiples and factors of numbers.

Materials
hundreds chart
colored marker

Students play this game in pairs as they circle factors or multiples of numbers until one player cannot select a number. They then analyze the strategies behind the game.

Answers
See Teacher Wraparound Edition p. 231.

Algebra Activity Recording Sheet
Analyzing Data
(p. 71 of this booklet)

Use With Lesson 5-8 as a preview activity. This corresponds to the activity on page 237 in the Student Edition.

Objective To collect data and analyze it using the mean, median, and mode.

Materials internet and/or newspapers optional

Students collect a group of data either by conducting a survey or by doing research. They summarize the data using a number that best describes all of the data in the set.

Answers
See Teacher Wraparound Edition p. 237.

Using Overhead Manipulatives

Mean, Median, and Mode
(p. 72 of this booklet)

Use With Lesson 5-8.

Objective To use the mean, median, and mode of numbers to analyze data.

Materials
counters*
small bowl
student calculators
blank transparency
transparency pens*
* = available in Overhead Manipulative Resources Kit

• The teacher demonstrates how to find the mean, median, and mode for a set of data after recording the number of counters taken from a bowl several times. There is a discussion of how measures of central tendency are affected by changing one number in the set.

• The extension activity asks students to explain why the mean is most affected by the addition of another number to the set of data.

Answers
Answers appear on the teacher demonstration instructions on page 72.

Mini-Project

Mean Deviation
(p. 73 of this booklet)

Use With Lesson 5-8.

Objective To calculate the mean deviation of a set of data in order to examine the variability of the set.

Materials
calculator with statistics functions, if available

Students work in small groups to calculate the mean and mean deviation for sets of data.

Answers
1. 85; 3.2
2. 84; 5.6
3. 19; 24
4. 35.6; 2.4
5. 13; 2.7
6. 50; 24.4
7. 80.8; 8.9
8. 2.7; 0.6
9. Answers will vary.
10. One that is widely spaced.

Algebra Activity

Analyzing Data
(p. 74 of this booklet)

Use With Lesson 5-8.

Objective To use a frequency table to calculate measures of central tendency.

Materials
none

Students construct a frequency table for a set of data and use it to calculate the mean, median, mode, and range of the data.

Answers
1.

Interval	Tally	Frequency
16–17	IIII	4
18–19	HHT III	8
20–21	HHT IIII	8
22–23	II	2
24–25	III	3

2. 19.8

3. 20

4. 18

5. 16

6. 25

7. 9

8. Sample: the mean because there is a small range of values.

Mini-Project
Adding Numbers in a Sequence
(p. 75 of this booklet)

Use With Lesson 5-10.

Objective To compute sums of arithmetic sequences.

Materials
none

Students work in small groups to examine the parts of an arithmetic sequence. They then calculate the sums of arithmetic sequences.

Answers
1. $0.80
2. $16.40
3. 3147
4. 210
5. 25
6. 1288

Algebra Activity
Triangular and Square Numbers
(pp. 76–77 of this booklet)

Use With Lesson 5-10.

Objective To use sequences to investigate triangular and square numbers.

Materials
geoboard pattern

Students work with geoboard patterns to draw figures that represent triangular and square numbers. They then compute values of sequences to draw conclusions about the relationship between the two.

Answers
1. 1, 1; 2, 3; 3, 6; 4, 10; 5, 15
2. $T_{n-1} + n$
3. 1, 1; 3, 4; 5, 9; 7, 16; 9, 25
4. $S_{n-1} + 2(n) - 1$
5. 4; 4

6. 9; 9
7. 16; 16
8. 25; 25
9. They are equal.

Using Overhead Manipulatives
Fibonacci Sequence
(p. 78 of this booklet)

Use With Lesson 5-10 as a follow-up activity.

Objective To investigate patterns in the Fibonacci sequence.

Materials
overhead projector calculator, if available
student calculators
blank transparency
transparency pen*
* = available in Overhead Manipulative Resources Kit

- The teacher shows students the first five terms in the Fibonacci sequence and then students find successive terms. A table is constructed to show what each term is divisible by and conjectures are made about the relationship between term number and divisibility.

- The extension activity asks students to begin a Fibonacci sequence on a different number and find a pattern between this sequence and the original one.

Answers
Answers appear on the teacher demonstration instructions on page 78.

Algebra Activity Recording Sheet
Fibonacci Sequence
(p. 79 of this booklet)

Use With Lesson 5-10 as a follow-up activity. This corresponds to the activity on page 253 in the Student Edition.

Objective To collect and analyze data concerning the quotient relationships in the Fibonacci sequence.

Chapter 5

Materials
artichoke, pineapple, or pinecone, marker

Students will collect data about the number of spiral rows on either an artichoke, pineapple, or pinecone. They will relate this data to the Fibonacci sequence, as well as find relationships between this sequence and the quotients of its successive terms. Students have the opportunity to conduct research on the golden ratio.

Answers
See Teacher Wraparound Edition p. 253.

Algebra Activity

(Use with Lesson 5-2)

Fractions

Materials: tangram (p. 23)
scissors

Below are two copies of a tangram. Cut out one copy and use the other copy as a model.

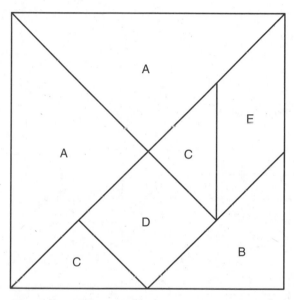

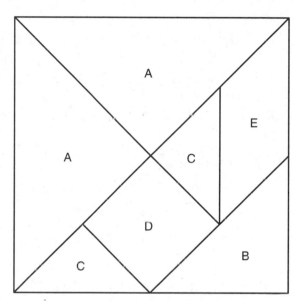

If the large square has an area of 1 square unit, give the area of each of the pieces.

1. Start with the pieces labeled **A**. The area of **A** is ___?___.

2. Compare piece **B** with piece **A**. The area of **B** is ___?___.

3. Compare the pieces labeled **C** with piece **B**. The area of **C** is ___?___.

4. Compare pieces **D** and **E** with **C**. The area of **D** is ___?___ and the area of **E** is ___?___.

5. Use the pieces to show:

   a. $2 \times \frac{1}{8}$

   b. $\frac{1}{4} \div \frac{1}{16}$

Chapter 5

Algebra Activity Recording Sheet

(Use with the Lesson 5-6 Follow-up activity on page 231 in the Student Edition.)

Juniper Green

Materials: hundreds chart, colored markers

Analyze the Strategies

Play the game several times using the grids below and then answer the following questions. Use the back of this sheet if you need more space.

1. Why do you think it is a rule that the first player must select an even number? Explain.

2. Describe the kinds of moves that were made just before the game was over.

1	2	3	4	5	6	7	8	9	10
11	12	13	14	15	16	17	18	19	20
21	22	23	24	25	26	27	28	29	30
31	32	33	34	35	36	37	38	39	40
41	42	43	44	45	46	47	48	49	50
51	52	53	54	55	56	57	58	59	60
61	62	63	64	65	66	67	68	69	70
71	72	73	74	75	76	77	78	79	80
81	82	83	84	85	86	87	88	89	90
91	92	93	94	95	96	97	98	99	100

1	2	3	4	5	6	7	8	9	10
11	12	13	14	15	16	17	18	19	20
21	22	23	24	25	26	27	28	29	30
31	32	33	34	35	36	37	38	39	40
41	42	43	44	45	46	47	48	49	50
51	52	53	54	55	56	57	58	59	60
61	62	63	64	65	66	67	68	69	70
71	72	73	74	75	76	77	78	79	80
81	82	83	84	85	86	87	88	89	90
91	92	93	94	95	96	97	98	99	100

1	2	3	4	5	6	7	8	9	10
11	12	13	14	15	16	17	18	19	20
21	22	23	24	25	26	27	28	29	30
31	32	33	34	35	36	37	38	39	40
41	42	43	44	45	46	47	48	49	50
51	52	53	54	55	56	57	58	59	60
61	62	63	64	65	66	67	68	69	70
71	72	73	74	75	76	77	78	79	80
81	82	83	84	85	86	87	88	89	90
91	92	93	94	95	96	97	98	99	100

1	2	3	4	5	6	7	8	9	10
11	12	13	14	15	16	17	18	19	20
21	22	23	24	25	26	27	28	29	30
31	32	33	34	35	36	37	38	39	40
41	42	43	44	45	46	47	48	49	50
51	52	53	54	55	56	57	58	59	60
61	62	63	64	65	66	67	68	69	70
71	72	73	74	75	76	77	78	79	80
81	82	83	84	85	86	87	88	89	90
91	92	93	94	95	96	97	98	99	100

Algebra Activity Recording Sheet

(Use with the activity on page 237 in Lesson 5-8 Preview of the Student Edition.)

Analyzing Data

Materials: none

Analyze the Data

1. Use the data you have collected and summarize it with a number that best describes all of the data in the set.

2. Explain what your number means, and explain which method you used to choose your number.

3. Describe how your number might be useful in real life.

Using Overhead Manipulatives

(Use with Lesson 5-8)

Mean, Median, and Mode

Objective Use the mean, median, and mode of numbers to analyze data.

Materials

- transparency pens*
- counters*
- small bowl
- student calculators
- blank transparency

* = available in Overhead Manipulative Resources Kit

Demonstration
Finding Measures of Central Tendency

- Place all the counters in a small bowl. Reach in and pull out a handful. Show students and ask them to estimate the number in your hand.

- Place the counters on the overhead and count them. Record the number on the transparency. Replace in the bowl and pull out another handful.

- Repeat until you have counted and recorded the number of counters in at least five handfuls.

- Have students use their calculators to add the data. Then have them divide the sum by the number of handfuls. Tell students that this number is called the *mean*. List the mean on the transparency.

- Below the original data, list the data in order from least to greatest. Ask students which number is in the middle. Circle this number. If there is no middle number, circle the middle two numbers and have students find their mean. Tell them that this number is called the *median* of the data. List the median on the transparency.

- Ask students whether one number in the set of data appears more often than the others. Tell them that this number, if there is one, is the *mode* of the data. List the mode, if there is one, on the transparency.

- Add the number 3 to the set of data. Ask students to predict which measure of central tendency will be affected the most. **mean**

- Then find the mean, median, and mode of the new set of data.

- Ask which measure of central tendency best represents the data before adding 3. Then ask which measure of central tendency best represents the data after adding 3. **mean, median, or possibly mode; median**

- Change the 3 to 300 and ask the same questions. **The answers will be the same.**

Extension
How the Mean is Affected

Ask students to explain why the mean was most affected by the data you added. **Since all the original data are close in number, the median is not affected much; the mode is not affected at all. The mean is most affected because it depends on the sum of the data.**

Mini-Project

(Use with Lesson 5-8)

Mean Deviation

Work in small groups. If you have access to a calculator that has statistical keys for finding the mean, you may use it.

Sometimes data from a survey or experiment vary, or deviate, a great deal. Other times the data are closely grouped.

The **mean deviation** is a measure of the variability of a set of data.

The table at the right gives the heights in inches of seven students. The mean (or average) height is 62 inches. The entries in the last column are the differences between each height and the mean.

Student	Height	Difference from Mean
Amy	60	2
Bob	63	1
Chad	61	1
Dan	67	5
Eve	58	4
Fran	62	0
Greg	63	1

To get Amy's difference from the mean:

$62 - 60 = 2$

To get Bob's difference from the mean:

$63 - 62 = 1$

The mean deviation is the mean of the numbers in the last column.

$$\frac{2 + 1 + 1 + 5 + 4 + 0 + 1}{7} = \frac{14}{7} = 2$$

Find the mean for each set of data. Then find the mean deviation. Round the mean and the mean deviation to the nearest tenth.

1. 80, 90, 82, 85, 88

2. 84, 94, 70, 87, 85

3. 3, 8, 2, 91, 4, 6

4. 34.4, 38.1, 39.0, 30.8, 35.7

5. 8, 12, 16, 12, 12, 18

6. 14, 100, 60, 25, 51

7. 80, 92, 76, 85, 90, 88, 84, 42, 86, 85

8. 2.1, 3.6, 2.5, 1.9, 3.3, 2.4, 3.6, 2.2

9. Find the heights, to the nearest inch, of all the members of your class. Find the mean deviation for the heights.

10. Is the mean deviation greater for a set of data that is widely spaced or for one that is closely grouped?

Chapter 5

Algebra Activity
(Use with Lesson 5-8)

Analyzing Data

The points scored by the high scorer for each basketball game played on one weekend in Allen County are given below.

```
16   18   22   20   18
17   19   23   18   16
21   18   25   21   20
21   18   20   20   18
24   17   19   21   25
```

1. Make a frequency table for this set of data.

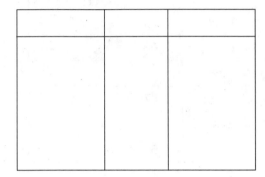

2. What is the mean?

3. What is the median?

4. What is the mode?

5. What is the lowest number of points scored?

6. What is the highest number of points scored?

7. Subtract the lowest number of points from the highest number of points. What is the range?

8. Which "average" best represents the typical highest number of points? Give a reason for your answer.

Mini-Project

(Use with Lesson 5-10)

Adding Numbers in a Sequence

Work in small groups. Study together the story below about Art. Then solve the problems at the bottom of the page.

Sixty days ago Art began to save pennies in a piggy bank. He saved two pennies the first day. Then each day afterward he saved one penny more than on the previous day. On the sixtieth day, he placed 61 pennies in the bank. He thought, "How can I find how much I have in the bank without adding $2 + 3 + \cdots + 60 + 61$?"

Art cleverly devised a short cut. He studied a pattern for finding the sum for 4 days. He said, "If I add

$$2 + 3 + 4 + 5$$
$$\text{to } 5 + 4 + 3 + 2$$

I get $7 + 7 + 7 + 7$, which is $4(7)$ or 28.

Then, $2 + 3 + 4 + 5$ must be half of 28, or 14. So in 4 days I saved 14 pennies. This means that

$$2 + 3 \ + \ldots + 60 + 61$$
$$\text{plus } 61 + 60 + \ldots + 3 \ + 2$$
$$\text{is } 63 + 63 + \ldots + 63 + 63, \text{ which is } 60(63) \text{ or } 3780.$$

Half of 3780 is 1890. So I must have saved 1890 pennies, or \$18.90."

Notice that $60(63)$ is equal to $60(2 + 61)$.

What Art discovered was a way to find the sum of the numbers in an arithmetic sequence if the first term, the last term, and the number of terms are known. If a is the first number of an arithmetic sequence, z is the last number, and n is the number of terms, then the sum S is found by the following formula.

$$S = \frac{1}{2}n(a + z)$$

1. Art's sister, Maggie, decided to save 2 pennies the first day. Then each day afterward she saved 2 pennies more than the previous day. If she saved for 40 days, how much did she save on the fortieth day?

2. How much did Maggie save in 40 days?

3. Find the sum of the numbers in the sequence 512, 517, 522, 527, 532, 537.

4. Find the sum of the first 20 counting numbers 1, 2, 3, ..., 20.

5. How many numbers are in the sequence 4, 8, 12, ..., 100?

6. Find the sum of the numbers in the sequence 12, 16, 20, ..., 100.

Teaching Pre-Algebra with Manipulatives

Chapter 5

Algebra Activity

(Use with Lesson 5-10)

Triangular and Square Numbers

Materials: geoboard pattern

Triangular and square numbers had great meaning for the ancient Greeks. Use the tables on this and the following page and the following notation to help discover the patterns for these numbers. Draw the figures on the geoboard pattern.

T refers to a triangular number.

S refers to a square number.

n refers to any term in the sequence. $n - 1$ is the term <u>before</u> the nth term. $n + 1$ is the term <u>after</u> the nth term.

1. Fill in the table to determine the first five triangular numbers.

n	Number of Dots Added	Total Number of Dots
1 •		$T_1 = \underline{?}$
2		$T_2 = \underline{?}$
3		$T_3 = \underline{?}$
4		$T_4 = \underline{?}$
5		$T_5 = \underline{?}$

2. What is the value of T_n?

3. Fill in the table to determine the first five square numbers.

n	Number of Dots Added	Total Number of Dots
1 •		$S_1 = \underline{?}$
2		$S_2 = \underline{?}$
3		$S_3 = \underline{?}$
4		$S_4 = \underline{?}$
5		$S_5 = \underline{?}$

4. What is the value of S_n?

Find each value.

5. $T_1 + T_2$; S_2

6. $T_2 + T_3$; S_3

7. $T_3 + T_4$; S_4

8. $T_4 + T_5$; S_5

9. What is the relationship between $T_{n-1} + T_n$ and S_n?

Teaching Pre-Algebra with Manipulatives

Chapter 5

Using Overhead Manipulatives

(Use with Lesson 5-10)

Fibonacci Sequence

Objective Investigate patterns in the Fibonacci sequence.

Materials
- overhead projector calculator, if available
- student calculators
- transparency pen*
- blank transparency

* = available in Overhead Manipulative Resources Kit

Demonstration
Patterns in the Fibonacci Sequence

- Write the first five terms in the Fibonacci sequence at the top of a blank transparency. Show students the pattern for finding each succeeding term (add the two preceeding terms) and use the pattern to find the 6th term.

$$
\begin{array}{cccccc}
 & & 1+1 & 1+2 & 2+3 & \mathbf{3+5} \\
1 & 1 & 2 & 3 & 5 & \textbf{\textit{(8)}}
\end{array}
$$

- Have students find the next four terms. **13, 21, 34, 55**

- Write the 7th through 10th terms on the transparency. Have students help as you add the next five terms to the list. **89, 144, 233, 377, 610**

- Use a colored transparency pen to underline every third number in the sequence. Ask students what the underlined terms have in common. **They are all divisible by 2.** Repeat for every 4th, 5th, and 6th terms. Make a chart on the transparency like the one shown below and use it to record answers.

Term	3rd	4th	5th	6th
Divisible by	*(2)*	*(3)*	*(5)*	*(8)*

- Ask students what number they think may be a factor of every seventh term. They may use calculators to check their conjectures. **13**

Extension
Altering the Sequence

Tell students that a Fibonacci sequence can begin at any number. Write the numbers 2, 2, 4, on a blank transparency. Have students use mental math and/or a calculator to tell what the next 10 terms would be. Ask students to compare this sequence with the original sequence and determine whether the same patterns hold. **6, 10, 16, 26, 42, 68, 110, 178, 288, 466; Each term in the second sequence is twice the corresponding term in the first sequence. The divisibility patterns hold for both sequences.**

Algebra Activity Recording Sheet

(Use with the Lesson 5-10 Follow-Up activity on page 253 in the Student Edition.)

Fibonacci Sequence

Materials: artichoke, pineapple, sunflower, or pinecone, marker

Analyze the Data

1. What do you notice about the number of rows in each item?

2. Compare your data with the data of the other groups. How do they compare?

Make a Conjecture

3. What is the relationship between the number of rows in sunflowers, pinecones, pineapples, and artichokes and the Fibonacci sequence?

Extend the Activity

4. Write the first fifteen terms in the Fibonacci sequence.

5. Divide each term by the previous term. Make a list of the quotients. If necessary, round to seven decimal places.

6. Describe the pattern in the quotients.

7. RESEARCH Find the definition of the **golden ratio**. What is the relationship between the numbers in the Fibonacci sequence and the golden ratio?

Chapter 5

- Students are divided into two teams and various spinners are used to record frequencies of sums and products. Students must decide if the rules for each game played make it fair or unfair.
- The extension activity looks at the theoretical probabilities of sums and products and asks students to analyze ratios.

Answers

Answers appear on the teacher demonstration instructions on pages 92–93.

Algebra Activity Recording Sheet

Taking a Survey
(p. 94 of this booklet)

Use With Lesson 6-9 as a preview activity. This corresponds to the activity on page 309 in the Student Edition.

Objective Identify sampling techniques and the strengths and weaknesses of each one.

Materials
none

Answers
See Teacher Wraparound Edition p. 309.

Mini-Project

(Use with Lesson 6-1)

Classroom Interior Design

Work in small groups to redesign your classroom to make it a better place to learn, work, and study. Assign different tasks to the following groups. Each group should write a report of its recommendations.

A. A planning group to decide which projects need to be undertaken—keep in mind that other people also use the room.

B. Work groups to plan each project in detail.

C. An evaluation group to evaluate the work that has been done by the other groups—be sure that all suggestions are necessary and practical. Decide whether the group's suggestions are important enough to be presented to your school administration.

The following problems will suggest projects that the planning group might decide are to be undertaken. The work groups should consider the questions posed in their problem.

1. Do the walls need to be painted? If so, you will need to find the area of the walls that are to be painted. Also, find how much paint is necessary to cover the walls. Talk about the various kinds and colors of paint available.

2. Does the ceiling need to be redone? If the ceiling is painted, consider redoing it with acoustical tiles. Find out how many tiles would be needed to cover the ceiling. What are the advantages of acoustical tile?

3. Does the floor surface need to be redone? Consider various options, such as vinyl tile, carpet tile, and so on, in view of how the room is used.

4. Are the windows in need of repair? Do they need recaulking? If they are supposed to open, do they operate properly? Are the shades adequate?

5. Is the classroom lighting sufficient? Are more light fixtures needed? Are those in use appropriate for a math classroom?

6. Is the heating/cooling system adequate? Can any improvements be made in the control of heat in the classroom?

7. Is the furniture in the room sufficient? Are the desks functional and comfortable? Can desks or tables be used effectively for small group activities? Using a floor plan drawn to scale, design an arrangement of the furniture. Consider the best arrangement for the way the classes are conducted.

8. Does your classroom need more chalkboards? Find the area of the present chalkboards. What other equipment is needed for a math classroom? Consider pencil sharpeners, reference books, measuring devices such as rulers, tape measures, and so on. Make a list of any items that are needed.

Chapter 6

Using Overhead Manipulatives

(Use with Lesson 6-2)

Capture-Recapture

Objective Use proportions to estimate a population.

Materials

- centimeter grid transparency*
- lined paper transparency*
- transparency pen*
- dried beans or squares of paper
- small bag or bowl

* = available in Overhead Manipulative Resources Kit

Demonstration
Capture-Recapture Simulation

- On the lined paper transparency, prepare a chart like the one shown at the right.

- Tell students they are going to model estimating a population using the **capture-recapture** technique. Dried beans or squares of paper will represent rabbits and the bowl will represent the forest. Fill the bowl with dried beans or squares of paper. Ask a student to grab a small handful of beans or squares of paper and place them on the screen. Count the number of beans or squares selected and record this number. Explain that these represent the captured rabbits. Mark each bean or square of paper with an X on both sides. Return them to the bowl and mix well with the rest.

- Have another student take a small handful of beans or squares of paper from the bowl. Record the number of beans or squares of paper selected. Tell students this represents the number of rabbits captured. Count the

Original Number Captured:		
Sample	Number Recaptured	Number Tagged in Sample
A		
B		
C		
D		
E		
F		
G		
H		
I		
J		
Total		

number of beans or squares of paper that are marked with an X in the handful. Tell students that this represents the number of "tagged" rabbits recaptured. Record these numbers in the chart. Return all the beans or squares of paper to the bowl, mix, and repeat the recapture process nine more times.

- Have students find the total recaptured and the total tagged. Record in the chart. Have students use the proportion below to estimate the total number of beans or squares of paper in the bowl.

$$\frac{\text{original number captured}}{\text{number in bowl}} = \frac{\text{total tagged in samples}}{\text{total recaptured}}$$

- Count all the beans or squares of paper in the bowl. Ask students how the estimate compares to the actual number. **Will vary, but should be close.**

Extension
Centimeter Grid Simulation

- Prepare the centimeter grid transparency by randomly coloring a dot in about 100 of the squares. Show students the grid. Tell them that the dotted squares are similar to the tagged beans in the bowl. Use sheets of paper to block off all but a random 5 cm-by-5 cm region. Tell students this is similar to removing a handful of counters. Count and record the number of dotted squares in the sample. Repeat for a total of 5 different samples. Ask students to state a proportion you could use to estimate the total number of dotted squares.

$$\frac{\textbf{original number dotted}}{\textbf{number of squares}} = \frac{\textbf{total dotted in samples}}{\textbf{total squares in samples}}$$

- Remind students that they can find the total number of squares by multiplying the number of rows by the number of columns in the grid. **368**

- Have students use the proportion to estimate the number of dotted squares. **The answer should be close to 100.**

- Tell students that there are actually about 100 dotted squares. Ask whether their estimate is close to 100. If not, ask students to give possible explanations. **Sample answers: The dots were not randomly distributed. By chance we sampled areas with more or fewer dots than average.**

Chapter 6

Algebra Activity Recording Sheet

(Use with the Lesson 6-2 Follow-Up activity on page 275 in the Student Edition.)

Capture-Recapture

Materials: bag of dried beans, paper bag, permanent marker

Collect the Data
Step 1   Use the table at the right to record your data.

Analyze the Data
1. Use the following proportion to estimate the number of beans in the bag.

$$\frac{\text{original number captured}}{\text{total number in bag}} = \frac{\text{total number tagged}}{\text{total number recaptured}}$$

2. Count the number of beans in the bag. Compare the estimate to the actual number.

Make a Conjecture
3. Why is it a good idea to base a prediction on several samples instead of one sample?

4. Why does this method work?

Original Number Captured:		
Sample	Recaptured	Tagged
1		
2		
3		
4		
5		
6		
7		
8		
9		
10		
Total		

Algebra Activity

(Use with Lesson 6-5)

Percents, Fractions, and Circle Graphs

Materials: none

A marketing firm ran a survey to find out what type of music people liked best. They interviewed 1920 people. The results are given below.

480 people preferred country music.
800 people preferred classical music.
360 people preferred jazz.
160 people preferred rock music.
120 people preferred rap music.

1. What percent of the people surveyed preferred each type of music? Enter the percents in the table below.

Type of Music	Percent
Country	
Classical	
Jazz	
Rock	
Rap	

2. If you were starting a new radio station in the area where the survey was conducted, which type of music would you play, based on the results of the survey?

People often use charts to help others understand information. One type of chart that is frequently used is a circle graph.

3. Using the completed table on the previous page, convert each percent to a fraction. Enter the fractions in the table below.

Type of Music	Fraction
Country	
Classical	
Jazz	
Rock	
Rap	

(continued on the next page)

Chapter 6

4. Using the fractions in the table, find and label the appropriate sector (or sectors) for each type of music. Shade the regions for Jazz and Classical. All the sectors labeled **a** are equal to each other. All the sectors labeled **b** are equal to each other.

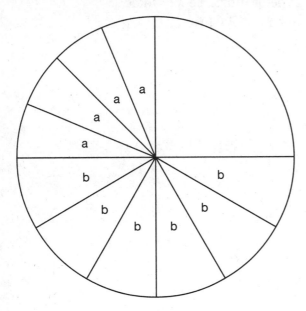

NAME _____ DATE _____ PERIOD ____

Algebra Activity Recording Sheet

(Use with the Lesson 6-5 Preview activity on pages 286–287 in the Student Edition.)

Using a Percent Model

Materials: grid paper

Activity 1

Draw a model and find the percent that is represented by each ratio. Estimate if necessary.

1. 6 out of 10

2. 9 out of 10

3. 2 out of 5

4. 3 out of 4

5. 9 out of 20

6. 8 out of 50

7. 2 out of 8

8. 3 out of 8

9. 2 out of 3

10. 5 out of 9

Activity 2

Draw a model and find the part that is represented. Estimate if necessary.

11. 10% of 50

12. 60% of 20

13. 90% of 40

14. 30% of 10

15. 25% of 20

16. 75% of 40

17. 5% of 200

18. 85% of 500

19. $33\frac{1}{3}$% of 12

20. 37.5% of 16
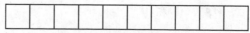

Chapter 6

Using Overhead Manipulatives

(Use with Lesson 6-6)

Making Predictions

Objective Conduct experiments to find experimental probability.

Materials
- lined paper transparency*
- transparency pen*
- paper bag
- 10 colored marbles or candies

* = available in Overhead Manipulative Resources Kit

Demonstration for Activity One
Sample Size 10

- On the lined paper transparency, prepare a chart like the one shown below.

Color	Tally	Relative Frequency

- Tell students that probability calculated by making observations or experiments is called **experimental probability.**

- Place all 10 marbles or candies in the bag. There should be at least three different colors. Show students the bag. Tell them that there are some different colored marbles or candies in the bag. Have a student draw one marble or candy from the bag. Record the color on the chart. Return the marble or candy to the bag. Repeat this 10 times.

- Explain that the term **relative frequency** means what fraction of the time a certain color is drawn. Ask students how they could calculate the relative frequency for each color. Have them calculate the relative frequency for each color and express it as a decimal. (If necessary, review how to express a fraction as a decimal.) Record in the chart. **Divide the number of times the color was drawn by ten; Answers will vary.**

- Based on the relative frequencies, which color marble do you think is most prevalent in the bag? Predict the colors of marbles in the bag. **Sample answer: Blue, because that is the color that was drawn most frequently.**

- Write the experimental probability of drawing each color marble using

the equation experimental probability $= \dfrac{\text{relative frequency of color}}{\text{total number of draws}}$.
Answers will vary.

Demonstration for Activity Two
Increased Sample Size

• Repeat the steps above for twenty, thirty, forty, and fifty draws.

• Is it possible to have a certain color marble or candy in the bag and never draw that color? Is this situation more likely to happen if you make two draws, ten draws, or fifty draws? Explain. **Yes; More likely to happen with two draws because if there are three or more colors in the bag you have not made enough draws to get every color once even if there were no repeats.**

• Compute the experimental probability of drawing each color for each number of draws. Describe how the experimental probability changed as you increased the number of draws. **Experimental probability becomes closer to the actual number of marbles or candies in the bag the more trials you conduct.**

• Predict the colors of the marbles or candies in your bag. Did your prediction change from the prediction you made in Activity 1? Open the bag and check your prediction against the contents. **Answers will vary.**

Extension
Making Predictions

Ask students how many times they would expect to draw each color if they made 1,000 draws. **Answers will vary.**

Chapter 6

Using Overhead Manipulatives

(Use with Lesson 6-6)

Fair and Unfair Games

Objective Determine whether a game is mathematically fair or unfair.

Materials
- spinners*, prepared as described below
- 2 blank transparencies*, prepared as described below
- transparency pens*

* = available in Overhead Manipulative Resources Kit

Demonstration
Games with Spinners

- Prepare the spinners as follows. First use the four-section spinner. Color three sections blue and one section green. Then use the six- and the three-section spinners. Draw lines on the three-section spinner to make six equal sections. Number the sections on each spinner 1–6.

- On a blank transparency, prepare a frequency table for sums like the one shown at the right. Also prepare an addition table as shown in the Extension on the next page.

- On a second blank transparency, prepare a frequency table for products as shown at the right. Also prepare a multiplication table as shown in the Extension on the next page.

- Say, "Suppose you and a friend are playing a game. In the game, you toss a coin. Each time the coin shows a head, you win. Each time the coin shows a tail, your friend wins. Do you both have an equal chance of winning? Why?" **Yes; the coin has one head and one tail, so the chance of each is the same.**

- Then say, "Suppose the game is changed to spinning a spinner like this one. (Show the four-section spinner with 1 green and 3 blue sections.) If the spinner lands in the green section, you win. If the spinner lands in the blue section, your friend wins. Do you both have an equal chance of winning? Why? **No; the blue section is much larger than the green section so your friend has a better chance of winning than you do.**

- Tell students that you are going to play some games with spinners and determine whether the games are fair. Clear the screen. Show students the six-section spinners you have prepared.

- Place the sum transparency on the screen so only the frequency table is showing.

Sum	Tally
2	
3	
4	
5	
6	
7	
8	
9	
10	
11	
12	

Product	Tally
1	
2	
3	
4	
5	
6	
8	
9	
10	
12	
15	
16	
18	
20	
24	
25	
30	
36	

- Divide the class into two teams. Call them Team X and Team Y. Tell them the rules for the game are as follows. "We will spin the spinners. If the sum of the two numbers is even, Team X gets a point. If the sum is odd, Team Y gets a point."

- Spin both spinners. Make a tally mark in the row next to the sum. Repeat until you have recorded 50 sums. Have members from each team count and report the number of points for their team. **Answers will vary; there should be about 25 for each.**

- Ask students whether they think this game is fair and why or why not. **This is a fair game. There are 12 ways to get an even-numbered sum and 12 ways to get an odd-numbered sum. However, this trial might not look fair. Accept any reasonable answers.**

- Clear the screen. Place the product transparency on the screen so only the frequency table is showing.

- Tell students that for this game, Team X gets a point for each *even* product and Team Y gets a point for each *odd* product.

- Spin both spinners. Make a tally mark in the row next to the product. Repeat until you have recorded 50 products. Have members of each team count and report the number of points for their team. **Answers will vary; there will be about 3 times as many even products as odd products.**

- Ask students whether they think this game is fair and why or why not. **Sample answer: The game is not fair because there are more ways to get an even product than to get an odd product.**

Extension
Show students an addition table like the one shown at the right. Ask the following questions. Which sum or sums from the addition table occur most often? Which sum or sums occur least often? Ask students to compare these answers to the tallies on the sum frequency table. **7; 2 and 12; They should be very similar.**

+	1	2	3	4	5	6
1	2	3	4	5	6	7
2	3	4	5	6	7	8
3	4	5	6	7	8	9
4	5	6	7	8	9	10
5	6	7	8	9	10	11
6	7	8	9	10	11	12

Show students a multiplication table like the one shown at the right. Ask whether even or odd products occur most often. Have students express the ratio of the number of odd products to the number of even products. Ask them to compare this ratio to the tallies on the product frequency table.

×	1	2	3	4	5	6
1	1	2	3	4	5	6
2	2	4	6	8	10	12
3	3	6	9	12	15	18
4	4	8	12	16	20	24
5	5	10	15	20	25	30
6	6	12	18	24	30	36

Chapter 6

Algebra Activity Recording Sheet

(Use with the Lesson 6-9 Preview activity on page 309 in the Student Edition.)

Taking a Survey

Materials: none

Model and Analyze

Tell whether or not each of the following is a random sample. Then provide an explanation describing the strengths and weaknesses of each sample.

	Type of Survey	Location of Survey
1.	travel preference	mall
2.	time spent reading	library
3.	favorite football player	Miami Dolphins football game

4. Brad conducted a survey to find out which food people in his community prefer. He surveyed every second person that walked into a certain fast-food restaurant. Identify this type of sampling. Explain how the survey may be biased.

5. Suppose a study shows that teenagers who eat breakfast each day earn higher grades than teenagers who skip breakfast. Tell how you can use the stratified sampling technique to test this claim in your school.

6. Suppose you want to determine where students in your school shop the most.

    a. Formulate a hypothesis about where students shop the most.

    b. Design and conduct a survey using one of the sampling techniques described above.

    c. Organize and display the results of your survey in a chart or graph.

    d. Evaluate your hypothesis by drawing a conclusion based on the survey.

Equations and Inequalities
Teaching Notes and Overview

Using Overhead Manipulatives

Solving Equations with Variables on Each Side
(pp. 97–98 of this booklet)

Use With Lesson 7-1.

Objective Use algebra tiles to model and solve equations with the variable on each side.

Materials
algebra tiles*
equation mat transparency*
transparency pen*
* = available in Overhead Manipulative Resources Kit

- This activity demonstrates the way to model equations with variables on each side using algebra tiles.
- The extension activity provides independent practice modeling and solving equations.

Answers
Answers appear on the teacher demonstration instructions on pages 97–98.

Algebra Activity Recording Sheet

Equations with Variables on Each Side
(p. 99 of this booklet)

Use With Lesson 7-1 as a preview activity. This corresponds to the activity on pages 328–329 in the Student Edition.

Objective Use algebra tiles to model and solve equations with variables on each side.

Materials
algebra tiles
equation mat

Students use algebra tiles and an equation mat to model and solve equations with variables on each side.

Answers
See Teacher Wraparound Edition pp. 328–329.

Algebra Activity

Solving Equations with Variables on Both Sides
(p. 100 of this booklet)

Use With Lesson 7-1.

Objective Use algebra tiles to model and solve equations with variables on both sides.

Materials
equation mat*
algebra tiles*
* = available in Overhead Manipulative Resources Kit

Students work with equation mats and algebra tiles to model and solve equations with variables on both sides.

Answers

1. Let x = number of sets: $2x + 1 = x + 5$ (Joan = Sergio); They have 4 sets of cards.

2. Let x = distance Sam lives from the shopping mall: $x = 1 = 3x - 7$ (Sam = Su-Lin); Sam lives 4 miles from the shopping mall. Su-Lin lives 5 miles from the shopping mall.

Algebra Activity

Inequalities and the Number Line
(p. 101 of this booklet)

Use With Lesson 7-4.

Objective Use a number line to graph solutions to compound inequalities.

Materials
none

Students work with compound inequalities. They will graph the solutions on number lines.

Answers

1.

2.

3.
```
←+++⊕++++●++→
  -2 -1  0  1  2  3  4
```

4.
```
←++●+++++○++→
   1  2  3  4  5  6  7
```

5.
```
←+++●+++++●+→
 -3 -2 -1  0  1  2  3
```

6.
```
←++⊕++++○+++→
   4     5     6     7
```

7. $x \geq 4.3$ and $x < 6.6$

8.
```
←++○+++++++⊕++→
   4      5      6      7
```

Using Overhead Manipulatives
(Use with Lesson 7-1)

Solving Equations with Variables on Each Side

Objective Use algebra tiles to model and solve equations with the variable on each side.

Materials
- algebra tiles*
- equation mat transparency*
- transparency pen*

* = available in Overhead Manipulative Resources Kit

Demonstration
Modeling Equations with Algebra Tiles

- Write the equation $2x - 6 = x - 3$ at the top of the mat transparency. Ask students how to model each side of the equality. Model the equation. **Place 2 x-tiles and 6 negative 1-tiles on the left side. Place an x-tile and 3 negative 1-tiles on the right side.**

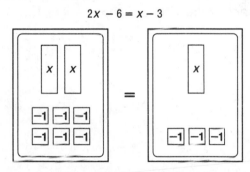

- Remind students that you can solve equations by removing an equal number of algebra tiles from each side in order to find the number of 1-tiles in an x-tile. Explain that for this equation you will remove both x- and 1-tiles.

- Ask students how many 1-tiles can be removed from each side. Remove 3 negative 1-tiles from each side. Then ask how many x-tiles can be removed from each side. Remove 1 x-tile from each side. Ask students to state the equation now shown. **3 negative 1-tiles; 1 x-tile from each side; x − 3 = 0**

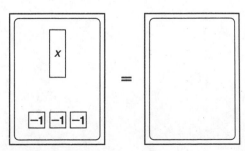

(continued on the next page)

• Add 3 zero pairs to the right side of the mat. Ask students why you have done this. Remove 3 negative 1-tiles from each side. Ask students what the value of x is in this equation. **You need to remove the 1-tiles on the left side, but there are no 1-tiles on the right side to match them with.; 3**

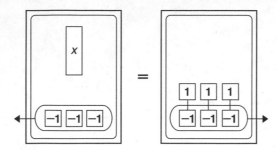

Extension
Modeling Practice
Model the equation $3x - 4 = x - 2$. Ask students to state the steps to solve the equation. **Remove 2 negative 1-tiles and one x-tile from each side. The equation is now $2x - 2 = 0$. Add 2 zero pairs to the right side of the mat. Then remove 2 negative 1-tiles from each side. The equation is now $2x = 2$. Match 1 positive 1-tile with each x-tile. The solution is $x = 1$.**

Algebra Activity Recording Sheet

(Use with the 7-1 Preview activity on pages 328–329 in the Student Edition.)

Equations with Variables on Each Side

Materials: algebra tiles, equation mat

Model
Use algebra tiles to model and solve each equation.

1. $2x + 3 = x + 5$

2. $3x + 4 = 2x + 8$

3. $3x = x + 6$

4. $6 + x = 4x$

5. $2x - 4 = x - 6$

6. $5x - 1 = 4x - 5$

7. $2x + 3 = x - 5$

8. $3x - 2 = x + 6$

9. $x - 1 = 3x + 7$

10. $x + 6 = 2x - 3$

11. $2x + 4 = 3x - 2$

12. $4x - 1 = 2x + 5$

Analyze
13. Does it matter whether you remove x tiles or 1 tiles first? Explain.

14. Explain how you could use models to solve $-2x + 5 = -x - 2$.

Algebra Activity

(Use with Lesson 7-1)

Solving Equations with Variables on Both Sides

Materials: equation mat, algebra tiles

Use *x*-tiles and l-tiles to model each situation. Then solve. Read each problem. Define a variable and write an equation.

1. Joan and Sergio both like to collect sets of baseball cards. They both have the same number of sets. If Joan doubles the number of sets she has and adds one more set, Sergio will need to buy five more sets to still have the same number of sets as Joan. How many sets do they both have now?

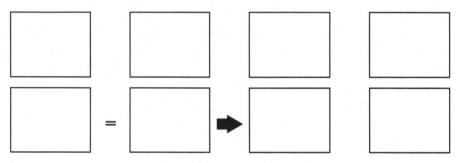

2. Sam and Su-Lin live on the same road. The road leads to a shopping mall. Sam lives closest to the mall. Su-Lin lives seven miles less than three times the distance that Sam lives from the mall. If you add one mile to the distance from Sam's house, it will be the same as the distance from Su-Lin's house. How far does each one live from the shopping mall?

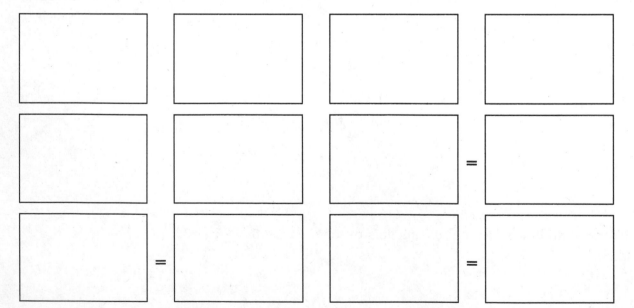

Algebra Activity

(Use with Lesson 7-4)

Inequalities and the Number Line

Materials: none

An **inequality** is a number sentence using greater than or less than. A **compound inequality** also uses the connection word <u>and</u> or <u>or</u>.

When the connecting word <u>and</u> is used, the solution set contains all the numbers that make *both* inequalities true.

$$x > 2.5 \text{ and } x < 5$$

When the connection word <u>or</u> is used, the solution set contains those numbers which make *either* inequality true.

$$x < 2.5 \text{ or } x > 5$$

Graph the solution for each compound inequality.

1. $x > 3.75$ <u>and</u> $x < 5.25$

2. $x > -2$ <u>and</u> $x < 1.3$

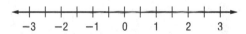

3. $x < -0.2$ <u>or</u> $x \geq 3.1$

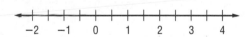

4. $x \leq 2$ <u>or</u> $x > 5.25$

5. $x \geq -1$ <u>and</u> $x \leq 2.75$

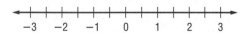

6. $x < 4.5$ <u>or</u> $x > 6.2$

Maria lives at least 4.3 miles from school and less than 6.6 miles from school. Use this information in Exercises 7 and 8.

7. Represent this distance as a compound inequality.

8. Graph the solution of the compound inequality on a number line.

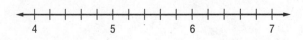

Functions and Graphing
Teaching Notes and Overview

Algebra Activity Recording Sheet
Input and Output
(p. 105 of this booklet)

Use With Lesson 8-1 as a preview activity. This corresponds to the activity on page 368 in the Student Edition.

Objective Explore functions by making and using a function machine.

Materials
two 3-by-5 inch index cards
scissors

Students will make a function machine with index cards. They will then use the function machine to find input and output values and write equations.

Answers
See Teacher Wraparound Edition p. 368.

Algebra Activity Recording Sheet
It's All Downhill
(p. 106 of this booklet)

Use With Lesson 8-4 as a preview activity. This corresponds to the activity on page 386 in the Student Edition.

Objective Explain how slope changes as height and length change.

Materials
posterboard
tape
books
toy car
yardstick

Students will run experiments with a toy car rolling down ramps of different heights and lengths to discover relationships about slope.

Answers
See Teacher Wraparound Edition p. 386.

Algebra Activity
Graphing and Slope
(p. 107 of this booklet)

Use With Lesson 8-4.

Objective To discover properties of horizontal and vertical lines and their graphs.

Materials
coordinate planes (p. 6)

Students graph ordered pairs and find the slopes between them to discover relationships about horizontal and vertical lines and their graphs.

Answers

1. Slopes for A are all 0; slopes for B are all none.

2. They are the same.

3. The slope of the lines connecting each pair of points in A is 0. The lines connecting each pair of points in B have no slope.

4. horizontal

5. vertical

Algebra Activity Recording Sheet
Slope and Rate of Change
(p. 108 of this booklet)

Use With Lesson 8-5 as a preview activity. This corresponds to the activity on page 392 in the Student Edition.

Objective Explore factors that affect the steepness of graphs and how this is related to rate.

Materials
water
drinking glass
ruler
tablespoon
$\frac{1}{4}$-cup measuring cup

Students perform an experiment in which the rate at which water is emptied from a glass is graphed. Comparisons are made between the steepness of graphs and conclusions are drawn about how this relates to rate.

Answers
See Teacher Wraparound Edition p. 392.

Using Overhead Manipulatives
Constant Rate of Change
(p. 109 of this booklet)

Use With Lesson 8-7.

Objective Show that the slope between any two points on a line is constant.

Materials
overhead grid transparency*
transparency pens*
* = available in Overhead Manipulative Resources Kit

• In this demonstration, students discover that the slope of a line is constant, that is, no matter which two points they choose on the line the slope between them will always be the same.

• The extension activity asks students to prove the linearity of a line by finding the slope between several sets of ordered pairs.

Answers
Answers appear on the teacher demonstration instructions on page 109.

Mini-Project
Writing Inequalities
(p. 110 of this booklet)

Use With Lesson 8-10.

Objective Write, graph, interpret, and find solutions for linear inequalities.

Materials

Students work in small groups to write inequalities for given situations. They then graph the inequalities, find ordered pairs that are solutions, and interpret the graphs.

Answers

Ordered pairs will vary. Sample pairs are given.

1. $y \leq 600 - x$; (200, 300); 200 yards can be used for Annie dolls, 300 yards can be used for Andy dolls.

2. $y \leq 40 - x$; (10, 20); Randy can spend 10 hours weaving rugs and 20 hours weaving placemats.

3. $y \leq 500 - 2x$; (100, 200); Lou can buy 100 lined pads and 200 unlined pads.

4. $y \geq 300 - x$; (200, 200); The company can send 200 lawnmowers to Ohio and 200 to Indiana.

Algebra Activity Recording Sheet

(Use with the Lesson 8-1 Preview activity on page 368 in the Student Edition.)

Input and Output

Materials: two 3-by-5 inch index cards, scissors

Make a Conjecture

1. Slide the function machine down so that the input is -4. Find the output and write the number in the right window. Continue this process for the remaining inputs.

2. Suppose x represents the input and y represents the output. Write an algebraic equation that represents what the function machine does.

3. Explain how you could find the input if you are given a rule and the corresponding output.

4. Determine whether the following statement is *true* or *false*. Explain. The input values depend on the output values.

5. Write an equation that describes the relationship between the input value x and the output value y in each table.

Extend the Activity

6. Write your own rule and use it to make a table of inputs and outputs. Exchange your table of values with another student. Use the table to determine each other's rule.

Algebra Activity Recording Sheet

(Use with the Lesson 8-4 Preview activity on page 386 in the Student Edition.)

It's All Downhill

Materials: posterboard, tape, books, yardstick, toy car

Collect the Data

Record your measurements in the table below.

Hill	Height y (in.)	Length x (in.)	Car Distance (in.)	Slope $\frac{y}{x}$
1				
2				
3				

Analyze the Data

1. How did the slope change when the height increased and the length decreased?

2. How did the slope change when the height decreased and the length increased?

3. **Make a Conjecture** On which hill would a toy car roll the farthest— a hill with slope $\frac{18}{25}$ or $\frac{25}{18}$? Explain by describing the relationship between slope and distance traveled.

Extend the Activity

4. Make a fourth hill. Find its slope and predict the distance a toy car will go when it rolls down the hill. Test your prediction by rolling a car down the hill.

Algebra Activity

(Use with Lesson 8-4)

Chapter 8

Graphing and Slope

Materials: coordinate planes

Slope is defined as the change in y divided by the change in x. Certain types of lines will always have the same slope. If the change in y is zero, the line has a slope of zero. If the change in x is zero, the line has no slope.

1. Graph the following pairs of points. Find the slope of the line that connects each pair of points. Record the results in the table.

A. Points	A. Slope	B. Points	B. Slope
$(-5, 3)$, $(7, 3)$ $(1, 5)$, $(7, 5)$ $(-2, 1)$, $(3, 1)$ $(0, 6)$, $(6, 6)$ $(-5, 4)$, $(1, 4)$		$(-5, 3)$, $(-5, 7)$ $(5, 1)$, $(5, 7)$ $(1, -2)$, $(1, 3)$ $(6, 0)$, $(6, 6)$ $(4, -5)$, $(4, 1)$	

2. What do you notice about the y-coordinate in each pair of points for **A**? the x-coordinate in each pair of points for **B**?

3. What is the slope of the lines connecting each pair of points in **A**? of the lines connecting each pair of points in **B**?

4. Let a represent any number. The equation for the lines in **A** is $y = a$. Is $y = a$ the equation for a vertical line or a horizontal line?

5. The equation for the lines in **B** is $x = a$. Is $x = a$ the equation for a vertical line or a horizontal line?

Algebra Activity Recording Sheet

(Use with the Lesson 8-5 Preview activity on page 392 in the Student Edition.)

Slope and Rate of Change

Materials: water, drinking glass, ruler, tablespoon, $\frac{1}{4}$-cup measuring cup

Collect the Data

Record your measurements in the table below.

Number of Measures	Height of Water (cm)	
	Tablespoons	**Cups**
0	(initial height)	(initial height)
1		
2		
3		
4		
5		
6		

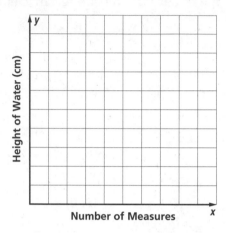

Analyze the Data

1. On the grid above, graph the ordered pairs (number of measures, height of water) for each set of data. Draw a line through each set of points. Label the lines 1 and 2, respectively.

Use the back of this sheet of paper to record your answers for Exercises 2–7 in your textbook.

Extend the Activity

8. Draw a graph of the water level in each of the containers as a function of time.

a.

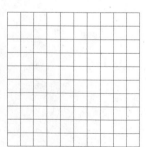

b.

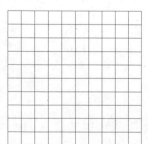

c.

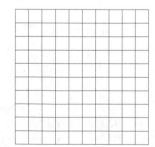

Using Overhead Manipulatives
(Use with Lesson 8-7)

Constant Rate of Change

Objective Show that the slope between any two points on a line is constant.

Materials
- overhead transparency grid*
- transparency pens*

* = available in Overhead Manipulative Resources Kit

Demonstration
Showing Slope is Constant

- Shows students the graph of a line with points at $(-2, 3)$ and $(1, 0)$. Ask them to find the slope of the line using these two points in the formula

  $m = \dfrac{\text{change in } y}{\text{change in } x}$. **−1**

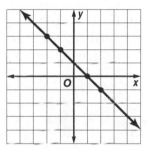

- Tell students that another point on this line is $(2, -1)$. Ask them to predict what the slope of the line between $(2, -1)$ and $(1, 0)$ will be. **−1**

- Find the slope between $(2, -1)$ and $(1, 0)$. **−1**

- Another point on the line is $(-1, 2)$. Find the slope between $(-2, 3)$ and $(-1, 2)$. **−1**

- Ask students what they can conclude about the slope between any two points on the line. **The slope will be −1.**

- Explain that a property of linear functions is that there is a constant rate of change. This is evidenced by the constant slope.

Extension
Proof of Linearity
Using the slopes between three different pairs of ordered pairs from the line at the right, show that this is a linear function. **Slope between each set of ordered pairs is $\frac{1}{2}$. Since there is a constant slope, it is a linear function.**

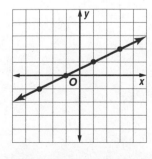

![people icon]

Mini-Project

(Use with Lesson 8-10)

Writing Inequalities

A cereal company has 300 pounds of almonds. The company uses *x* pounds of almonds in its Happy Trails cereal and *y* pounds of almonds in its Fruity Nuts cereal.

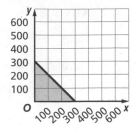

After *x* pounds of nuts are used in Happy Trails, 300 − *x* pounds of almonds are available for Fruity Nuts. You can write an inequality to represent this relationship.

$y \leq 300 - x$

An ordered pair that is a solution of the inequality is (100, 150). This means that the company can use 100 pounds of almonds in Happy Trails and 150 pounds of almonds in Fruity Nuts.

Work in small groups. Write an inequality for *y* for each situation. Then graph the inequality on the grid below it. Find an ordered pair that is a solution of the inequality and tell what it means.

1. A toy company has 600 yards of material for its rag dolls. The company uses *x* yards of material for its Annie dolls and *y* yards of material for its Andy dolls.

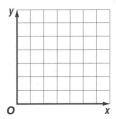

2. Randy weaves rugs and place mats on a loom that she rents for 40 hours each week. She spends *x* hours weaving rugs and *y* hours weaving place mats each week.

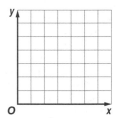

3. Lou has $500 to spend on lined and unlined notepads for the bookstore. He buys *x* lined pads for $2 each and *y* unlined pads for $1 each.

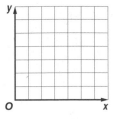

4. A company must ship 300 lawnmowers or more each month. It will ship *x* lawnmowers to its warehouse in Ohio and *y* lawnmowers to its warehouse in Indiana.

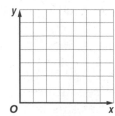

Chapter

9 Real Numbers and Right Triangles
Teaching Notes and Overview

Using Overhead Manipulatives

Subsets of the Real Number System
(p. 114 of this booklet)

Use With Lesson 9-2.

Objective Classify numbers into the subsets of the real number system using a Venn diagram.

Materials
4 blank transparencies, prepared as described
transparency pen*
* = available in Overhead Manipulative Resources Kit

- This demonstration shows students how the subsets of the real number system are related to each other using a Venn diagram.
- The extension activity asks students to turn this information into a concept map.

Answers
Answers appear on the teacher demonstration instructions on page 114.

Algebra Activity Recording Sheet

The Pythagorean Theorem
(p. 115 of this booklet)

Use With Lesson 9-5 as a preview activity. This corresponds to the activity on pages 458–459 in the Student Edition.

Objective Find the area of various figures using dot paper and relate this to the Pythagorean Theorem.

Materials
none

Students draw figures on dot paper and use the grid to find the areas of the figures. They then relate area concepts to the Pythagorean Theorem.

Answers
See Teacher Wraparound Edition p. 458–459.

Algebra Activity

Pythagorean Triples
(p. 116 of this booklet)

Use With Lesson 9-5.

Objective Identify and investigate relationships with Pythagorean Triples.

Materials
calculator

Students first identify Pythagorean Triples. They then look for relationships between the triples and use these relationships to predict other Pythagorean Triples.

Answers

1. triple
2. not a triple
3. triple
4. not a triple
5. triple
6. triple
7. not a triple
8. triple
9. triple

Chapter 9

10. a. The second triple is the sum of the first triple and {3, 4, 5}.

b. The third triple is twice the first triple, or the sum of the first triple and 2 × {3, 4, 5}.

c. The fourth triple is the sum of the first triple and 3 × {3, 4, 5}.

11. They are multiples of the set {3, 4, 5}.

12. Yes; It is 10 × {3, 4, 5}.

13. Sample answers: {10, 24, 26}, {15, 36, 39}, {20, 48, 52}

Algebra Activity Recording Sheet

Graphing Irrational Numbers
(p. 117 of this booklet)

Use With Lesson 9-5 as a follow-up activity. This corresponds to the activity on page 465 in the Student Edition.

Objective Graph irrational numbers on a number line.

Materials
compass

Students use a compass and graph paper to construct triangles used to graph irrational numbers on a number line.

Answers
See Teacher Wraparound Edition p. 465.

Algebra Activity

Using the Pythagorean Theorem
(p. 118 of this booklet)

Use With Lesson 9-6.

Objective Use the Pythagorean Theorem to find the length of lines.

Materials
calculator

Students find the length of lines on a grid by turning them into right triangles and using the Pythagorean Theorem.

Answers

1. 2, 4, 5, 25, 29, 29, 5.39

2. 7, 49, 8, 64, 113, 113, 10.63

3. 3, 9, 4, 16, 25, 25, 5

4. 5, 25, 12, 144, 169, 169, 13

Algebra Activity

Similar Triangles, Indirect Measurement
(p. 119 of this booklet)

Use With Lesson 9-7.

Objective Use similar triangles and proportions to indirectly measure tall objects.

Materials
paper towel tube
stick
string
meterstick

Students construct stadias and use them to indirectly measure the heights of tall objects. This is done by solving proportions set up with similar triangles.

Answers

1. $\frac{0.9}{2} = \frac{x}{14}$; 6.3 m

2. Answers will vary.

Algebra Activity Recording Sheet

Ratios in Right Triangles
(p. 120 in this booklet)

Use With Lesson 9-8 as a preview activity. This corresponds to the activity on page 476 in the Student Edition.

Objective Discover the 30°-60°-90° and
45°-45°-90° triangle relationships.

Materials
ruler
protractor

Students draw triangles, measure the sides and
angles, and draw conclusions about the special
relationships in these triangles. They discover
30°-60°-90° triangles and 45°-45°-90° triangles.

Answers
See Teacher Wraparound Edition p. 476.

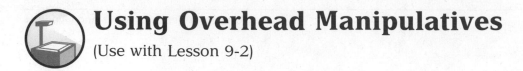

Using Overhead Manipulatives

(Use with Lesson 9-2)

Subsets of the Real Number System

Objective Classify numbers into the subsets of the real number system using a Venn diagram.

Materials

- 4 blank transparencies, prepared as described below
- transparency pen*

* = available in Overhead Manipulative Resources Kit

Demonstration
Constructing a Venn diagram

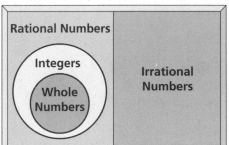

- Each transparency will be set up to overlay the others so that the end result will look like the picture at the right. The first transparency contains only a red circle for whole numbers. The next transparency contains a yellow circle for integers. The third has the rational numbers box, and the final transparency contains the irrational numbers box and the real numbers label.

- Say "We are going to construct a Venn diagram using the different types of numbers we are familiar with." Begin by displaying the whole numbers box. Ask students to give examples of whole numbers and write some of them inside the circle. **(0, 1, 2, 3, 4,...)**

- Display the yellow circle on top of the red circle. Name some numbers from the set of integers. Explain that since the red circle is contained in the yellow circle, all of the whole numbers are integers.

- Add the rational numbers box on top of the existing transparencies and ask students to give examples of numbers that fit into this category. Again emphasize that all of the integers (and consequently, whole numbers) are in the set of rational numbers. These numbers include terminating and repeating decimals and fractions. **Fractions and decimals; answers will vary, but a rational number is any number that can be expressed as the ratio of two integers where the denominator is not 0.**

- Explain that there are some decimals that do not fit in the category of rational numbers because they do not terminate and they do not repeat. These are called irrational numbers. Examples of irrational numbers include π and $\sqrt{2}$. Display the final transparency and explain that with the addition of irrational numbers we complete the real number system.

- Ask students why the irrational numbers are contained in a box rather than in a circle like the other categories. **The irrational and rational numbers are completely different sets with no overlapping elements.**

Extension
Concept Mapping

Construct a concept map that explains the subsets of the real number system and includes examples. **See students' work.**

Algebra Activity Recording Sheet

(Use with the Lesson 9-5 Preview activity on pages 458–459 in the Student Edition.)

The Pythagorean Theorem

Materials: none

Model

Find the area of each figure.

1. 　　2. 　　3. 　　4.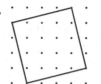

Use the table at the right to record your results for Activity 2.

	Area of Square A	Area of Square B	Area of Square C
Triangle #1			
Triangle #2			
Triangle #3			
Triangle #4			

Exercises

1. Refer to your table. How does the sum of the areas of square A and square B compare to the area of square C?

2. Tell whether each set of numbers is a Pythagorean Triple. Explain why or why not.
   a. 3, 4, 5　　　　**b.** 5, 7, 9　　　　**c.** 6, 9, 12　　　　**d.** 7, 24, 25

3. Write two different sets of numbers that are a Pythagorean Triple.

Chapter 9

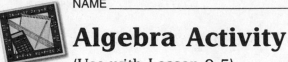

Algebra Activity

(Use with Lesson 9-5)

Pythagorean Triples

Materials: calculator

A **Pythagorean Triple** is a set of three whole numbers $\{a, b, c\}$ that could represent the lengths of the sides of a right triangle. In other words, the three numbers have the following relationship.

$$a^2 + b^2 = c^2$$

Check to see if the set $\{3, 4, 5\}$ is a Pythagorean Triple.

$$3^2 + 4^2 \stackrel{?}{=} 5^2$$

$$9 + 16 \stackrel{?}{=} 25$$

$$25 = 25$$

The set $\{3, 4, 5\}$ is a Pythagorean Triple.

Determine if each set of numbers is a Pythagorean Triple. Make a list of the Pythagorean Triples as you go through these exercises.

1. $\{6, 8, 10\}$ 2. $\{2, 3, 4\}$ 3. $\{9, 12, 15\}$

4. $\{8, 10, 12\}$ 5. $\{12, 16, 20\}$ 6. $\{15, 20, 25\}$

7. $\{20, 33, 30\}$ 8. $\{18, 24, 30\}$ 9. $\{36, 48, 60\}$

10. **a.** What is the relationship between the first Pythagorean Triple in your list and the second Pythagorean Triple?

   b. Between the first triple and the third Triple?

   c. Between the first triple and the fourth Triple?

11. What relationship do you see among the Pythagorean Triples in your list?

12. From your observations, do you think that the set $\{30, 40, 50\}$ is a Pythagorean Triple? Why? Verify your answer.

13. $\{5, 12, 13\}$ is a Pythagorean Triple. Use this information to write three other Pythagorean Triples.

Algebra Activity Recording Sheet

(Use with the Lesson 9-5 Follow-up activity on page 465 in the Student Edition.)

Graphing Irrational Numbers

Materials: compass

Model and Analyze

Use a compass to graph each irrational number.

1. $\sqrt{5}$

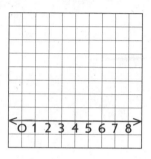

2. $\sqrt{20}$

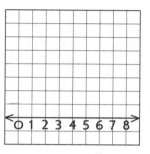

3. $\sqrt{45}$

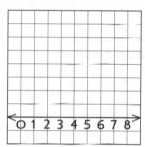

4. $\sqrt{97}$

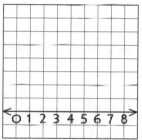

5. Describe two different ways to graph $\sqrt{34}$.

6. Explain how the graph of $\sqrt{2}$ can be used to locate the graph of $\sqrt{3}$.

Teaching Pre-Algebra with Manipulatives

Algebra Activity

(Use with Lesson 9-6)

Using the Pythagorean Theorem

Materials: calculator

Find the length of the lines using the Pythagorean Theorem. Draw
a right triangle for each line, using the line as the hypotenuse.
Then complete the table at the bottom.

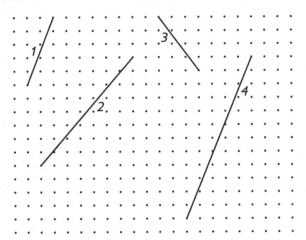

	Shorter Leg, a	a^2	Longer Leg, b	b^2	$a^2 + b^2$	c^2	c
1.							
2.							
3.							
4.							

Algebra Activity

(Use with Lesson 9-7)

Similar Triangles, Indirect Measurement

A **stadia** like the one shown at the right can be used to find the height of an object. Hold the stadia to your eye. Back away from the object until the top and the bottom of the object are in line with the strings. Then record the two readings where the strings appear to cross the stick. Measure the distance from the stadia to the stick and the distance from the stadia to the object. Notice that two similar triangles are formed.

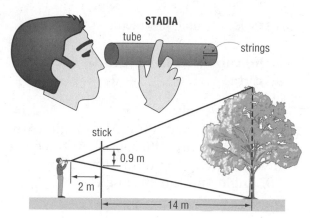

1. Set up a proportion and find the height of the tree shown in the diagram.

2. Use the stadia and a measuring stick to find the height of the following objects. Remember to measure the distances between yourself and the stick (Distance 1) and between yourself and the object (Distance 2). Record your data in the table below.

Object	Distance 1	Distance 2	Height
Building			
Tree			
Flagpole			

Chapter 9

Algebra Activity Recording Sheet

(Use with the Lesson 9-8 Preview activity on page 476 in the Student Edition.)

Ratios in Right Triangles

Materials: ruler, protractor

Use the tables at the right to record your data.

	30° angle	60° angle
Length (mm) of opposite leg		
Length (mm) of adjacent leg		
Length (mm) of hypotenuse		
Ratio 1		
Ratio 2		
Ratio 3		

Model and Analyze

1. Draw another 30°-60°-90° triangle with side lengths that are different than the one drawn in the activity. Then find the ratios for the 30° angle and the 60° angle.

2. **Make a conjecture** about the ratio of the sides of any 30°-60°-90° triangle.

3. Repeat the activity with a triangle whose angles measure 45°, 45°, and 90°. What can you conclude about the ratio of the sides of a 45°-45°-90° triangle?

	45° angle	45° angle
Length (mm) of opposite leg		
Length (mm) of adjacent leg		
Length (mm) of hypotenuse		
Ratio 1		
Ratio 2		
Ratio 3		

Two-Dimensional Figures
Teaching Notes and Overview

 ### *Algebra Activity Recording Sheet*

Constructions
(p. 126 of this booklet)

Use With Lesson 10-1 as a follow-up activity. This corresponds to the activity on pages 498–499 in the Student Edition.

Objective Use a compass and straightedge to construct bisectors.

Materials
compass
ruler

Students first use a compass and straightedge to construct congruent line segments and angles. They then use the compass to construct a perpendicular bisector of a line segment and a bisector of an angle.

Answers
See Teacher Wraparound Edition pp. 498–499.

 ### *Mini-Project*

Exploring Congruence
(p. 127 of this booklet)

Use With Lesson 10-2.

Objective Determine ways of showing that triangles are congruent.

Materials
ruler
scissors
paper
compass
protractor

Students work in three groups to construct triangles and determine ways of telling if the triangles are congruent.

Answers

1. See students' work.

2. See students' work.

3. See students' work.

4. The triangles for each group should match.

5. They are congruent.

6. They are congruent.

7. They are congruent.

 ### *Algebra Activity Recording Sheet*

Symmetry
(p. 128 of this booklet)

Use With Lesson 10-3 as a preview activity. This corresponds to the activity on page 505 in the Student Edition.

Objective Identify and draw lines of symmetry.

Materials
straightedge

Students will determine whether various figures have any lines of symmetry, and if so, they will draw them. Students will also explore the concept of rotational symmetry by turning figures to determine whether they have line symmetry, rotational symmetry, or both.

Answers
See Teacher Wraparound Edition p. 505.

Chapter 10

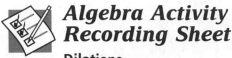

Algebra Activity Recording Sheet

Dilations
(p. 129 of this booklet)

Use With Lesson 10-3 as a follow-up activity. This corresponds to the activity on page 512 in the Student Edition.

Objective Use dilations to alter the size of figures.

Materials
grid paper
protractor
ruler

Students will draw new figures given a scale factor. They will then compare the two figures to determine whether the dilation is a reduction or an enlargement. Students will also compare dilations to other transformations, such as translations, rotations, and reflections.

Answers
See Teacher Wraparound Edition p. 512.

Using Overhead Manipulatives

Areas and Geoboards
(pp. 130–131 of this booklet)

Use With Lesson 10-5.

Objective Use a geoboard to find areas of shapes that are not rectangular.

Materials
geoboard*
geobands*
dot paper transparency*
transparency pens*
* = available in Overhead Manipulative Resources Kit

This demonstration consists of three activities.

- Demonstration 1 uses geoboards to find the areas of irregularly shaped figures.
- Demonstration 2 uses geoboards to show the relationship between the area of a rectangle and the area of a triangle.
- The extension activity asks students how to find the area of a triangle when it is not possible to form just one rectangle.

Answers
Answers appear on the teacher demonstration instructions on pages 130–131.

Algebra Activity Recording Sheet

Area and Geoboards
(p. 132 of this booklet)

Use With Lesson 10-5 as a preview activity. This corresponds to the activity on pages 518–519 in the Student Edition.

Objective Use geoboards to find areas of figures.

Materials
geoboard
rubber bands

Students will use geoboards to make figures and find their areas. They will also use the method of building a rectangle around right triangles and irregularly shaped figures to find their areas.

Answers
See Teacher Wraparound Edition pp. 518–519.

Using Overhead Manipulatives

Tessellations
(pp. 133–134 of this booklet)

Use With Lesson 10-6.

Objective Investigate tessellations using regular polygons.

Materials
regular polygons transparency*
blank transparency, prepared as described
transparency pens*
transparency of recording sheet as shown

- This demonstration shows students an example of a tessellation using equilateral triangles. Then it is shown that pentagons do not tessellate. This pattern is repeated for squares, hexagons, octagons, and dodecagons. Students calculate the sum of the angle measures for each regular polygon.

- The extension activity shows how cutting a part off one side of a square and taping it to the opposite side will still allow the figure to tessellate.

Answers
Answers appear on the teacher demonstration instructions on pages 133–134.

Algebra Activity Recording Sheet

Tessellations
(p. 135 of this booklet)

Use With Lesson 10-6 as a follow-up activity. This corresponds to the activity on page 532 in the Student Edition.

Objective Use transformations to form tesselations.

Materials
none

Students will use various types of transformations to create tessellations for given pattern units.

Answers
See Teacher Wraparound Edition p. 532.

Using Overhead Manipulatives

Circles and Slope
(pp. 136–137 of this booklet)

Use With Lesson 10-7

Objective Use cylindrical objects to discover a connection between algebra and geometry.

Materials
centimeter grid transparency*, prepared as described below
small cylindrical objects less than 7 cm in diameter, such as a vitamin bottle, a salt shaker, a tuna can, and a soup can
matchstick or small strip of paper
tape
straightedge*
* = available in Overhead Manipulative Resources Kit

Chapter 10

- In this demonstration the teacher graphs the relationship between the diameter and circumference of cylindrical objects by rolling them on the grid paper.

- The extension activity ask students to predict the circumference of cylinders given the diameters.

Answers
Answers appear on the teacher demonstration instructions on pages 136–137.

Mini-Project

Exploring π
(p. 138 of this booklet)

Use With Lesson 10-7.

Objective Conduct an experiment that leads to an approximation of π.

Materials
paper
metric ruler
"stick" 1 centimeter long made from a flat toothpick

Students work in pairs to perform an experiment, record data, and graph approximations of π.

Answers
Answers will vary.

Algebra Activity

How Big is Your Foot?
(p. 139 of this booklet)

Use With Lesson 10-8

Objective Measure the areas of irregular regions and make comparisons.

Materials
centimeter grid*
* = available in Overhead Manipulative Resources Kit

Students use a centimeter grid to measure the area of irregular regions. They make comparisons between the length, width, and area of footprints as a person grows.

Answers

1. approximately 16 cm^2

2. approximately 70 cm^2

3. Answers will vary.

4. approximately twice as long, but answers will vary

5. a little less than twice as wide, but answers will vary

6. a little more than 4 times greater, but answers will vary

Using Overhead Manipulatives

Area and Perimeter
(p. 140 of this booklet)

Use With Lesson 10-8.

Objective Discover the greatest possible perimeter for a given area.

Materials
centimeter grid transparency*
centimeter grid paper
transparency pens*
* = available in Overhead Manipulative Resources Kit

- Students find the perimeter of several different figures with the same area. They then find the greatest possible perimeter.
- In the extension activity students find the greatest possible perimeter for a different given area. They describe how perimeter changes as shape changes.

Answers
Answers appear on the teacher demonstration instructions on page 140.

Algebra Activity Recording Sheet

(Use with the Lesson 10-1 Follow-Up activity on pages 498–499 in the Student Edition.)

Constructions

Materials: compass, ruler

Model and Analyze

1. Draw a line segment. Construct a line segment congruent to the one drawn.

2. Draw an angle. Construct an angle congruent to the one drawn.

3. In Activity 3, use a ruler to measure $\overline{XM}$ and $\overline{MY}$. This construction bisects a segment. What do you think *bisects* means?

4. Draw a line segment. Construct the perpendicular bisector of the segment.

5. In Activity 4, what is true about the measures of $\angle MNQ$ and $\angle QNP$?

6. Why do we say $\overrightarrow{NQ}$ is the bisector of $\angle MNP$?

Mini-Project

(Use with Lesson 10-2)

Exploring Congruence

Divide the class into three groups of equal size
Everyone may use a pencil, paper, ruler, and scissors.
Each member of group A may also use a compass.
Each member of groups B and C may also use a
protractor.

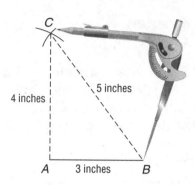

1. If you are a member of group A, draw $\triangle ABC$ so that $AB =$ 3 inches. Open the compass to a width of 4 inches, place the point at A, and mark an arc. Then open the compass to a width of 5 inches, place the point at B, and mark another arc. The intersection is point C. Draw $\triangle ABC$.

2. If you are a member of Group B, draw $\triangle PQR$ so that $PQ = 5$ inches, $m\angle Q = 60°$, and $QR = 6$ inches.

3. If you are a member of group C, draw $\triangle STU$ so that $m\angle U = 50°$, $TU = 8$ inches, and $m\angle T = 40°$.

4. Cut out the triangle that you drew. Compare it with the triangles drawn by other members of your group. Can your triangle be made to match every other triangle of your group by placing them on top of each other? Share your results with the rest of the class.

5. If the sides of one triangle are congruent to the sides of another triangle, what conclusion can you draw about the triangles?

6. If two sides of one triangle are congruent to two sides of another and the angles included between these sides are congruent, what conclusion can you draw about the triangles?

7. If two angles of one triangle are congruent to two angles of another triangle and the sides between the angles are congruent, what conclusion can you draw about the triangles?

Chapter 10

Algebra Activity Recording Sheet

(Use with the Lesson 10-3 Preview activity on page 505 in the Student Edition.)

Symmetry

Materials: straightedge

Activity 1

Draw a line down the center of the butterfly. Notice how the two halves match. When this happens, a figure is said to have **line symmetry**, and the line is called a *line of symmetry*. A figure that has line symmetry has **bilateral symmetry**.

Analyze

Determine whether each figure has line symmetry. If it does, draw all lines of symmetry. If not, write *none*.

1.

2.

3.

Activity 2

In the space below, draw what the figure looks like with each rotation.

original figure   90°   180°   270°

What do you notice about the appearance of the figure in each rotation?

ANALYZE

Determine whether each figure has rotational symmetry. Write *yes* or *no*.

4.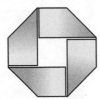

5.

6.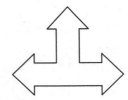

7. Name three objects that have both line symmetry and rotational symmetry.

Algebra Activity Recording Sheet

(Use with the Lesson 10-3 Follow-Up activity on page 512 in the Student Edition.)

Dilations

Materials: grid paper, protractor, ruler

Analyze the Data

1. Use a protractor to measure the angles in each trapezoid. How do they compare?

2. Use a ruler to measure the sides of each trapezoid. How do they compare?

3. What ratio compares the measures of the corresponding sides.

4. Repeat the activity by multiplying the coordinates of trapezoid *ABCD* by $\frac{1}{2}$. Are the results the same? Explain.

Make a Conjecture

5. Explain how you know whether a dilation is a reduction or an enlargement.

6. Explain the difference between dilations and the other types of transformations.

Extend the Activity

Find the coordinates of the dilation image for the given scale factor, and graph the dilation image.

7. 3 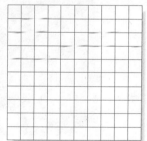 8. $\frac{1}{4}$ 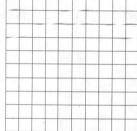 9. $1\frac{1}{2}$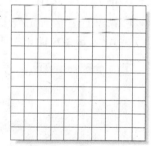

Identify each transformation as a *translation, rotation, reflection,* or *dilation*.

10.   11.   12.

Chapter 10

Using Overhead Manipulatives

(Use with Lesson 10-5)

Areas and Geoboards

Objective Use a geoboard to find areas of shapes that are not rectangular.

Materials
- geoboard*
- geobands*
- dot paper transparency*
- transparency pens*   * = available in Overhead Manipulative Resources Kit

---

Demonstration 1
Finding Areas of Irregular Shapes

- Review the meaning of area. Ask students to find the area of a rectangle. Point out that not all shapes are rectangles. **Multiply length × width.**

- Show students the figure on the geoboard at the right. Tell them that one square represents one square unit and ask them to find the area of the figure. Ask them how they found the area.
6 sq. units; Sample answer: Count the squares.

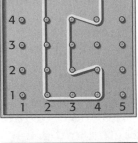

- Now make the second figure shown at the right. Ask students if they can count squares to find the area. Point out the half squares in the figure. Label each whole (1) and each half $\left(\frac{1}{2}\right)$ square. Then have students add to find the area. **no; 5 sq. units**

- Copy the figure on the dot paper transparency and record the area.

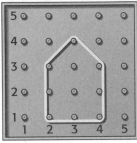

- Clear the geoboard. Repeat the previous two steps for the figures below. **3 sq. units; 8 sq. units**

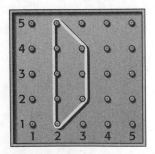 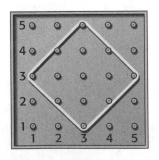

Demonstration 2
Relationship Between Triangles and Rectangles

- Make the triangle shown at the right on the geoboard. Point out that the triangle is not made of just whole and half squares.

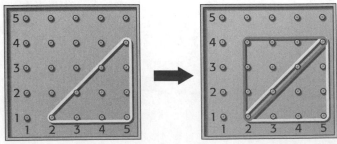

- Say, "Suppose we make another triangle just like it to form a rectangle." Use a different colored geoband to form the second triangle.
- Ask, "What is the area of the rectangle?" **12 sq. units**
- Ask, "How does the area of the rectangle compare to the area of the original triangle?" **It has twice the area.**
- Ask, "What is the area of the original triangle?" **6 sq. units**
- Copy the figure on the dot paper transparency and record its area.
- Repeat for the triangles shown at the right. **4 sq. units; 3 sq. units**
- Point out that all the triangles in this activity are right triangles. Ask a student to make a right triangle on the geoboard. Have the class find the area of the figure. **Answers will vary.**
- Ask students how they found the areas of the triangles. **Sample answer: Find the area of a rectangle with the same length sides and divide by 2.**

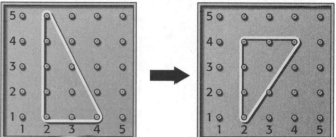

Extension
Including the Triangle
Make the triangle shown at the right on the geoboard. Point out that you cannot make a rectangle by using another triangle just like it. Ask students if there is any way to make a rectangle that includes the triangle. **Sample answer: Use one side of the triangle as a side of the rectangle. Then make a rectangle with the opposite vertex of the triangle on the rectangle.**

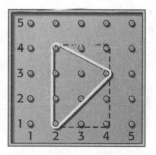

Make the rectangle. Have students find the area of the large rectangle and record it. Shade the original triangle. Label the "outside" triangles *a* and *b*. Ask how you could find the area of the original triangle. **Subtract the areas of triangles *a* and *b* from the area of the rectangle.**

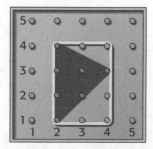

Point out that the outside triangles are right triangles and ask students how to find their areas. Record the areas of the outside triangles and subtract to find the area of the original triangle. **Make a rectangle and divide its area by 2; 3 sq. units**

Chapter 10

Algebra Activity Recording Sheet

(Use with the Lesson 10-5 Preview activity on pages 518–519 in the Student Edition.)

Area and Geoboards

Materials: geoboard, rubber bands

Model and Analyze

Find the area of each figure. Estimate if necessary.

1. 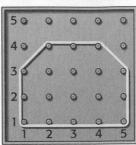   2. 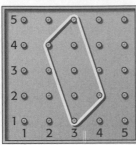   3.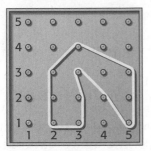

4. Explain how you found the area of each figure in Exercises 1–3.

5. Make a figure on the geoboard. Ask a classmate to find the area of the figure.

Find the area of each triangle.

6. 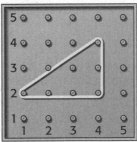   7. 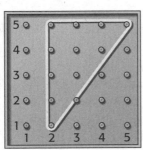   8.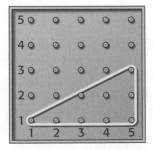

9. Make a right triangle on your geoboard. Ask a classmate to find its area using this method.

10. Write a few sentences explaining how you found the area of the triangle.

Find the area of each figure by building a rectangle around the figure.

11.    12. 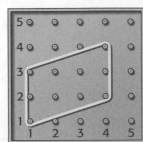   13.

14. Make a figure on your geoboard. Ask a classmate to find the area using this method.

Using Overhead Manipulatives

(Use with Lesson 10-6)

Tessellations

Objective Investigate tessellations using regular polygons.

Materials
- regular polygons transparency*
- blank transparency, prepared as described below
- blank transparencies*
- transparency pens*

* = available in Overhead Manipulative Resources Kit

Demonstration
Constructing Tessellations

- Prepare a transparency as follows. Place the polygon transparency under a blank transparency. Trace the equilateral triangle. Turn the top transparency so that the two triangles share a common side. Trace the second triangle. Continue this process until a pattern becomes obvious.

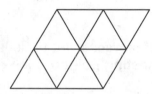

- Show students the prepared transparency. Tell students that this is an example of a **tessellation**. Explain that in a tessellation, the shapes fit together with no holes or gaps. Ask what shape you used. **equilateral triangle**

- Point out the regular pentagon on the polygon transparency. Ask students if they think a tessellation can be made using the pentagon. Use tracings to show that the pentagon does not tessellate.

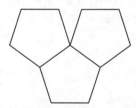

- Repeat for the square, regular hexagon, regular octagon, and regular dodecagon. **The square and hexagon will tessellate, the octagon and dodecagon will not.**

- Remind students that if a polygon has n sides, the sum of the degree measures of its angles is $(n - 2)180$. Have students calculate the sum of the angle measures for each regular polygon. Then have them determine the measure of one angle in each regular polygon. **180°, 360°, 540°, 720°, 1080°, 1800°; 60°, 90°, 108°, 120°, 135°, 150°**

- Record the results in a table like the one on the next page. *(continued on the next page)*

Figure	Sum of Angle Measures	Measure of One Angle
Equilateral Triangle		
Square		
Regular Pentagon		
Regular Octagon		
Regular Dodecagon		

- How can you tell from the measure of one angle whether or not a single polygon will tessellate? **If 360 is a multiple of the angle's measure, it will tessellate.**

- Try to make tessellations for each of these combinations:

  a. square and octagon

  b. square, triangle, and hexagon

  c. square, triangle, and dodecagon

  d. another combination you choose

- How can you tell whether a combination of polygons will tessellate? **If the sum of the angle measures at each meeting point of the vertices is 360°, it will tessellate.**

Extension
Transforming a Square
Draw a square on a blank transparency. Change the top side by drawing an angle as shown. Then erase the top of the square. Translate the angle to the bottom of the square. Erase the bottom of the square. Ask students whether they think this shape will tessellate and why. **Yes; squares tessellate and these squares were changed by taking a shape from the top and adding it to the bottom, so each bottom shape will fit exactly in the top of the next piece.**

Algebra Activity Recording Sheet

(Use with the Lesson 10-6 Follow-up activity on page 532 in the Student Edition.)

Tessellations

Materials: none

Model

Use a translation to create a tessellation for each pattern unit shown.

1.   2.   3.

Use a rotation to create a tessellation for each pattern unit shown.

4.   5.   6.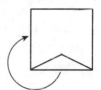

7. Make a tessellation that involves a translation, a rotation, or a combination of the two.

Chapter 10

Using Overhead Manipulatives

(Use with Lesson 10-7)

Circles and Slope

> **Objective** Use cylindrical objects to discover a connection between algebra and geometry.
>
> **Materials**
> - centimeter grid transparency, prepared as described below
> - small cylindrical objects less than 7 cm in diameter, such as a vitamin bottle, a salt shaker, a tuna can, and a soup can
> - matchstick or small strip of paper
> - tape
> - straightedge*   * = available in Overhead Manipulative Resources Kit

Demonstration
Diameter and Circumference of Cylinders

- Prepare the centimeter grid transparency by labeling coordinate axes as shown below.

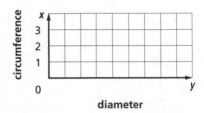

- Display the coordinate axes and point out the labels. Tell students that you are going to graph the relationship between the diameter and circumference of cylindrical objects. Review the meanings of diameter and circumference.

- Place one of the cylinders on the grid with its base on the horizontal axis, its left edge at the origin and with half of the cylinder on either side of the horizontal axis. Point out that the point where the right side of the base crosses the horizontal axis is the measure of the diameter of the cylinder. Leave the cylinder on the grid.

- Rotate the cylinder about the point on the horizontal axis so it is resting on its side as shown.

- Carefully tape the matchstick or strip to the side of the cylinder at the point where it rests on the horizontal axis. Tell students that the stick will mark a beginning and end for measuring the circumference of the cylinder.

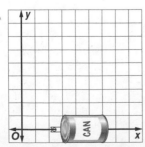

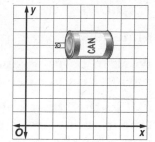

- Roll the cylinder up the grid parallel to the vertical axis one complete rotation. (The stick will come into focus when it again lies on the screen.) Mark the point where the cylinder rests on the grid paper. Ask students to name the ordered pair for the point. Record the ordered pair in the upper right corner of the transparency.

- Repeat this procedure with a different cylindrical object.

- Draw a line through the two points marked on the grid paper.

- Estimate the slope of the line using ordered pairs. Then determine the slope of the line. **Slope should be about 3.**

- Where would you expect a point to be if you repeated the above procedure with a third cylindrical object? **The point should be on the line.**

- Using what you know about circles and circumference, what should the slope of the line be? Explain your reasoning. **Sample answer: The slope should equal π because the change in *y* is the circumference and the change in *x* is the diameter and circumference divided by diameter is π. The slope is about 3.14.**

Extension
Predicting Circumference
Repeat the activity using a different cylinder whose diameter is between those used above. Ask students to predict the circumference of the cylinder after you have measured its diameter. Check the predictions by rolling the cylinder on the grid. Repeat with a cylinder whose circumference is greater than or less than the cylinders on the original graph.

Chapter 10

Mini-Project

(Use with, Lesson 10-7)

Exploring π

Materials: paper, a metric ruler, a "stick" 1 centimeter long made from a flat toothpick

Work in pairs. Prepare for the following experiments by drawing parallel lines 2 centimeters apart across a piece of paper.

Fill in the chart below by performing each experiment as follows: One student drops the stick on the paper the number of times given for the experiment. The other student records the number of times the stick lands on a line. Divide the number of times the stick is dropped by the number of times the stick lands on a line. Record the quotient, which is an approximation for π.

	Experiment	Number of times stick is dropped	Number of times stick lands on a line	Approximation of π
1.	A	30 times		
2.	B	40 times		
3.	C	50 times		
4.	D	60 times		
5.	E	70 times		

6. Complete the graph below using the results from Experiments A–E.

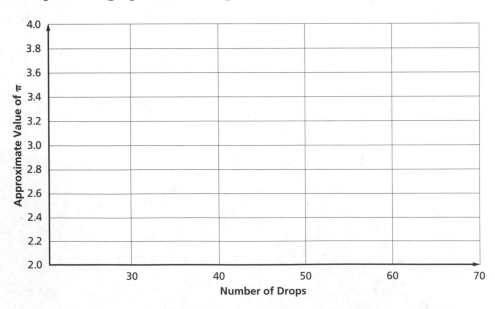

7. Do the points seem to cluster around one value of π? If so, what is that value?

8. Find the average of the approximations of π found by Experiments A–E.

Algebra Activity

(Use with Lesson 10-8)

How Big is Your Foot?

Materials: centimeter grid, pencil

In this activity, you use a centimeter grid to measure the area of an irregular region, and then explore how the length, width, and area of footprints change as a person grows.

1. A one-month-old baby's foot has been measured and found to be 4 centimeters wide and 8 centimeters long. Draw an approximate foot shape on the graph paper that is 8 centimeters long and 4 centimeters wide. Estimate the area by counting the squares the foot covers, including the total of all the partial squares.

2. A four-year-old child's foot has been measured and found to be 15 centimeters long and 7 centimeters wide. Draw an approximate foot shape on the graph paper that is 15 centimeters long and 7 centimeters wide. Estimate the area by counting the squares the foot covers, including the total of all the parts of squares.

3. Trace your own foot on the centimeter grid and find the following.

   a. length

   b. width

   c. approximate area

4. Compare the baby's foot to the child's foot. Compare your foot to both of the others.

   a. How many times longer is the child's foot than the baby's foot? How does your foot compare to the baby's foot?

   b. How many times wider is the child's foot than the baby's foot? How does your foot compare to the baby's foot?

   c. How much greater is the approximate area of the child's foot than the baby's foot? How does your foot compare to the baby's foot?

Chapter 10

Using Overhead Manipulatives

(Use with Pre-Algebra, Lesson 10-8)

Area and Perimeter

> **Objective** Discover the greatest possible perimeter for a given area.
>
> **Materials**
> • centimeter grid transparency
> • centimeter grid paper
> • transparency pens*   * = available in Overhead Manipulative Resources Kit

Demonstration
Finding Greatest Possible Perimeter

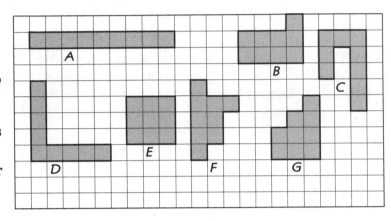

• Tell students that you are going to draw several figures with areas of 9 square units. On the centimeter grid transparency, copy the shapes shown at the right.

• Ask students to find the perimeter of each figure. Record each perimeter outside the figure. Ask students what appears to be the greatest possible perimeter for an area of 9 square units. **A = 20 units, B = 14 units, C = 20 units, D = 20 units, E = 12 units, F = 16 units, G = 14 units; 20 units**

• Have students find the greatest possible perimeter for areas of 8, 10, and 15 square units. They should draw a figure to show the greatest possible perimeter. **18 units; 22 units; 32 units**

• A figure has an area of 50 square units. Predict the greatest possible perimeter. **102 units**

• Explain why the two figures at the right have the same perimeter. Draw another figure with the same perimeter. **The squares still share the same number of sides.**

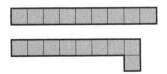

• Suppose a figure has an area of x square units. Write an expression for the greatest possible perimeter. **2x + 2 units**

Extension
Relationship Between Perimeter and Shape

• On centimeter grid paper, have students draw *rectangular* shapes using exactly 20 squares of the grid.

• Ask students to find the perimeter of each rectangle. **1-by-20, P = 42 cm; 2-by-10, P = 24 cm; 4-by-5, P = 18 cm**

• Ask students to describe how the perimeter changes as the shape changes. **It decreases as the shape becomes more like a square.**

Three-Dimensional Figures
Teaching Notes and Overview

Geometry Activity Recording Sheet

Building Three-Dimensional Figures
(p. 143 of this booklet)

Use With Lesson 11-1 as a preview activity. This corresponds to the activity on pages 554–555 in the Student Edition.

Objective Sketch top, front, and side views of geometric figures. Work with nets.

Materials
scissors
tape
isometric dot paper
grid paper

Students sketch models of the front, top, and side views of three-dimensional figures on isometric dot paper. They then cut out and fold nets as well as draw sketches of these figures.

Answers
See student work.

Geometry Activity Recording Sheet

Volume
(p. 144 of this booklet)

Use With Lesson 11-2 as a preview activity. This corresponds to the activity on page 562 in the Student Edition.

Objective Investigate volumes by making containers of different shapes and comparing how much each container holds.

Materials
three 5 × 8 index cards
rice
tape

Answers
See Teacher Wraparound Edition p. 562.

Using Overhead Manipulatives

Volume
(pp. 145–146 of this booklet)

Use With Lesson 11-5.

Objective Investigate volume by making containers of different shapes and comparing how much each container holds.

Materials
six 3-by-5 index cards
tape
bag of small beans
blank transparency
ruler*
centimeter grid transparency*
transparency pens*
counters*
algebra tiles*
* = available in Overhead Manipulative Resources Kit

- In this demonstration, three containers are made from index cards, and students estimate the quantity of beans that will fit in each one. There is a discussion of how the heights, the perimeters of the bases, and the areas of the bases compare in order to determine a relationship between base area and volume.

- The extension activity investigates why products are not usually packaged in circular containers even though a circular base seems to hold the most for a given height.

Answers
Answers appear on the teacher demonstration instructions on pages 145–146.

Chapter 11

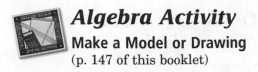

Algebra Activity
Make a Model or Drawing
(p. 147 of this booklet)

Use With Lesson 11-5.

Objective Draw nets for container designs and evaluate them based on their volumes.

Materials
scissors
graph paper
tape
construction paper

Students work in groups to construct nets for various figures. They must determine the best net to use based on volume contained.

Answers

1. squares, triangles

2. pyramid

3. Answers will vary.

4. See students' work.

5. See students' work.

Geometry Activity
Recording Sheet
Similar Solids
(p. 148 of this booklet)

Use With Lesson 11-6 as a preview activity. This corresponds to the activity on page 583 in the Student Edition.

Objective Investigate similar solids and scale factor.

Materials
sugar cubes

Students calculate the surface area and volume of sugar cubes in order to learn about scale factor and similar solids.

Answers
See Teacher Wraparound Edition p. 583.

Geometry Activity Recording Sheet

(Use with the Lesson 11-1 Preview Activity on pages 554–555 in the Student Edition.)

Building Three-Dimensional Figures

Materials: isometric dot paper, grid paper, scissors, tape

Model

1–6. Draw your models on isometric dot paper.

7–9. Draw your views on grid paper.

Cut out each net and fold on the dashed lines to make a 3-dimensional figure, using the shaded areas as the bases.

10.

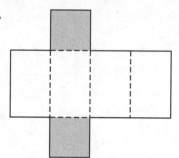

11.

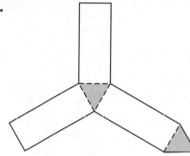

12.

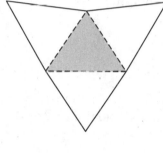

13.

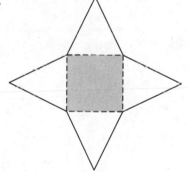

14.

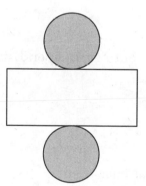

15.

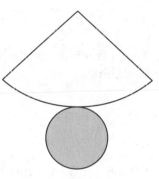

Sketch each figure and draw and label the top view, a side view, and the front view.

10.   **11.**   **12.**

13.   **14.**   **15.**

© Glencoe/McGraw-Hill

143

Teaching Pre-Algebra with Manipulatives

Chapter 11

Geometry Activity Recording Sheet

(Use with the Lesson 11-2 Preview Activity on page 562 in the Student Edition.)

Volume

Materials: three 5 × 8 index cards, tape, rice

Analyze the Data

1. Which container holds the greatest amount of rice? Which holds the least amount?

2. How do the heights of the three containers compare? What is each height?

3. Compare the perimeters of the bases of each container. What is each base perimeter?

4. Trace the base of each container onto grid paper. Estimate the area of each base.

5. Which container has the greatest base area?

6. Does there appear to be a relationship between the area of the bases and the volume of the containers when the heights remain unchanged? Explain.

Using Overhead Manipulatives

(Use with Lesson 11-5)

Volume

Objective Investigate volume by making containers of different shapes and comparing how much each container holds.

Materials
- six 3-by-5 index cards
- tape
- bag of small beans
- blank transparency
- ruler*
- centimeter grid transparency*
- transparency pens*
- counters*
- algebra tiles*

* = available in Overhead Manipulative Resources Kit

Demonstration
Relating Base Area and Volume

- Use the 3×5 cards to make three containers. Explain that each figure has a height of 3 inches. Make one with a square base, one with a triangular base, and one with a circular base. To make the cylinder, roll the card up several times to help it stay round. Fold a card in half twice to make a square prism. The triangular prism requires two folds of a card.

- Tape one end of each container to another card as a bottom, but leave the top open.

- Ask students to estimate which container will hold more beans, which will hold less, or whether they will all hold the same amount. **circular, most; triangular, least**

- Place one of the containers on the screen and fill it with beans. Place another container on the screen and carefully pour the beans from the first container into the second. If the second container holds less, students will see that some of the beans spill over the top. If the second container holds more, show students that it is not full. Record on the blank transparency, for example, circular > square. Repeat with the third container and record the results. (If you started with the triangular container, you may need to repeat the activity to compare the square and circular containers. If you started with the circular container, you may need to repeat to compare the triangular and square containers. **circular, most; triangular, least**

(continued on the next page)

Chapter 11

- Ask, "How do the heights of the three containers compare?" You may need to remind them that the shapes were made from 3-inch by 5-inch cards. You may also lay each container on its side next to the overhead ruler to find its height. **same height; 3 in.**

- Then ask, "What is the perimeter of the base of each container?" If necessary, remind students of the size of the card, or you may want to use the ruler to measure the sides to find the perimeter. Place the centimeter grid transparency on the screen. Trace the open top (base) of each container onto the grid. Ask students how they could estimate the area of each base. **same perimeter; 5 in.; possible answers include counting squares and partial squares within the figure; and counting units to estimate the measure of sides, height, or diameter and then using formulas to estimate the areas**

- Estimate each area. **triangle: about 8 cm^2; square: a little more than 9 cm^2; circle: a little more than 12 cm^2**

- Ask, "Which container has the greatest base area? **cylinder**

- Ask students if there seems to be a relationship between the area of each base and the amount of beans the container will hold. **The greater the base area, the greater the volume.**

Extension
Circular Packaging
Ask students why, when a circular base seems to hold the most for a given height, most products are not packaged in circular containers. Use counters to represent circular containers and area tiles to represent square and rectangular containers. Place the models on the centimeter grid transparency to show how much space is unused when packing circular containers as compared to square or rectangular containers. **Answer may vary.**

Algebra Activity

(Use with Lesson 11-5)

Make a Model or Drawing

Materials: scissors, graph paper, tape, construction paper

A solid with at least one flat surface can be formed from a pattern called a **net**.

Work in groups.
Draw the figure below on graph paper. What geometric figure forms the parts of this net?

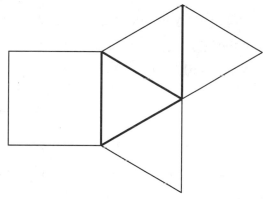

Cut out the figure and fold it along the heavy lines. Tape the edges together to form a solid.

1. What solid was formed when the edges were taped together?

2. Sketch the solid. Compare your sketch with others done by your group. What similarities and differences do you see?

3. Study the solid. Is there another net that would produce this solid? If so, draw it.

For a fund-raising project, junior high students are selling popcorn at the basketball game. Your class has been asked to design the containers that will hold 2 cups of popcorn. The containers can be shaped like a rectangle or a cylinder, or another shape that would be easy to hold.

Work with your group to draw a net for the container design. Then cut it out of construction paper and test its sturdiness. If possible, get two cups of popcorn to test the volume the container can hold.

Chapter 11

Geometry Activity Recording Sheet

(Use with the Lesson 11-6 Preview Activity on page 583 in the Student Edition.)

Similar Solids

Materials: sugar cubes

Activity 1

Analyze the Data

1. How many small cubes did you use? _____

2. What is the area of one face of the original cube? _____

3. What is the area of one face of the cube that you built? _____

4. What is the volume of the original cube? _____

5. What is the volume of the cube that you built? _____

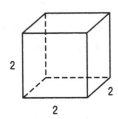

Activity 2

Analyze the Data

6. How many small cubes did you use? _____

7. What is the area of one face of the cube? _____

8. What is the volume of the cube? _____

9. Complete the table at the right.

10. What happens to the area of a face when the length of a side is doubled? tripled?

Scale Factor	Side Length	Area of a Face	Volume
1			
2			
3			

11. Considering the unit cube, if the scale factor is x, what is the area of the face? the surface area?

12. What happens to the volume of a cube when the length of a side is doubled? tripled?

13. Considering the unit cube, let the scale factor be x. Write an expression for the cube's volume.

14. **Make a conjecture** about the surface area and the volume of a cube if the sides are 4 times longer than the original cube.

15. **RESEARCH** the scale factor of a model car. Use the scale factor to estimate the surface area and volume of the actual car.

More Statistics and Probability
Teaching Notes and Overview

Algebra Activity Recording Sheet

Probability and Pascal's Triangle
(p. 151 of this booklet)

Use With Lesson 12-6 as a follow-up activity. This corresponds to the activity on page 640 in the Student Edition.

Objective Explore and find probabilities using tree diagrams and Pascal's Triangle.

Materials
none

Students will draw tree diagrams illustrating all the possible outcomes of tossing various coins. They will then compare these outcomes to Pascal's Triangle.

Answers
See Teacher Wraparound Edition p. 640.

Mini-Project

Music Hath Charms
(p. 152 of this booklet)

Use With Lesson 12-7.

Objective Use Venn diagrams to display and discuss survey results.

Materials
none

Students work in small groups to conduct a class survey about music preferences. They then construct a Venn diagram and use it to discuss survey results.

Answers

1. students who enjoy rock, but not rhythm and blues and not country-western

2. students who enjoy rhythm and blues, but not rock and not country-western

3. students who enjoy country-western, but not rock and not rhythm and blues

4. students who enjoy rock and rhythm and blues, but not country-western

5. students who enjoy rock and country-western, but not rhythm and blues

6. students who enjoy rhythm and blues and country-western, but not rock

7. students who enjoy all three types of music

8. students who do not enjoy any of the three types of music

9. the number of students in the class

10–17. Answers will vary.

Using Overhead Manipulatives

Permutations and Combinations
(pp. 153–154 of this booklet)

Use With Lesson 12-7.

Objective Explore and use permutations and combinations.

Materials
transparency pen*
blank transparency cut into ten rectangular "cards"
2 blank transparencies
* = available in Overhead Manipulative Resources Kit

This demonstration contains three activities.

• Demonstration 1 models a permutation by having students stand in a line at the front of the room. They then use cards to talk about the possibilities of rearranging the order of students. Permutations are also made with various multi-digit numbers.

• Demonstration 2 uses pizza toppings to model different combinations of choices. The difference between a permutation and a combination is discussed.

Chapter 12

- The extension activity asks students to name other examples of permutations and combinations.

Answers

Answers appear on the teacher demonstration instructions on pages 153–154.

Algebra Activity

Punnett Squares
(p. 155 of this booklet)

Use With Lesson 12-6.

Objective Use Punnett squares to examine combinations of genetic traits.

Materials
integer mat
algebra tiles
counters

Answers

1.

2. RRYY, RRYy, Rryy, RrYY, Rryy, rrYY, rrYy, rryy

3. 9

4. 3

5. 3

6. 1

Mini-Project

Verifying Probability by Experiment
(p. 156 of this booklet)

Use With Lesson 12-9.

Objective Compute experimental and theoretical probabilities.

Materials
number cube

Students work in groups to calculate the theoretical probability for each roll of a number cube. They then roll a number cube 60 times and calculate experimental probability.

Answers

1–4. $\frac{1}{6}$

5–18. Answers will vary.

Algebra Activity Recording Sheet

Simulations
(p. 157 of this booklet)

Use With Lesson 12-9 as a follow-up activity. This corresponds to the activity on pages 656–657 in the Student Edition.

Objective Use simulations to model problems involving probability.

Materials
number cube
coin
two colors of counters
two colors of marbles

Students conduct several simulations in order to calculate experimental probability. They model questions on a true-false test using coin tosses, fast-food restaurant prizes with a number cube, and free throws with marbles and counters.

Answers
See Teacher Wraparound Edition pp. 656–657.

Algebra Activity Recording Sheet

(Use with the Lesson 12-6 Follow-up Activity on page 640 in the Student Edition.)

Probability and Pascal's Triangle

Materials: none

Collect Data

Make a tree diagram for tossing the coins listed.

penny and dime	penny, nickel, and dime
Penny H T Dime H T H Outcomes H,H ___ ___ ___	

penny, nickel, dime, and quarter

For Exercises 1–9, write your answers on the back of this sheet.

Chapter 12

Mini-Project

(Use with Lesson 12-7)

Music Hath Charms

Work in small groups. Conduct a survey of your class to determine how many of your classmates enjoy rock music, rhythm and blues, and country-western music.

Use a Venn diagram like the one at the right to help you organize your data. The total of the numbers in the top left circle should be the number of students who like rock music; the total in the top right circle should be the number who like rhythm and blues; and the total in the bottom circle should be the number who like country-western.

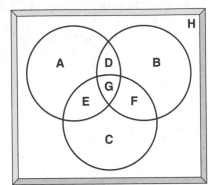

Which groups are represented by the following regions?

1. A

2. B

3. C

4. D

5. E

6. F

7. G

8. That part of H not in any circle

9. What should the total of all the numbers in the rectangle represent?

Use your Venn diagram to answer the following.

10. How many students enjoy rock music, but not rhythm and blues and not country-western?

11. How many students enjoy both rhythm and blues and country-western, but not rock?

12. How many students enjoy all three types of music?

13. How many do not like any of the three types?

14. How many enjoy rock and country-western, but not rhythm and blues?

15. How many enjoy country-western, but not rock and not rhythm and blues?

16. How many enjoy rhythm and blues, but not rock and not country-western?

17. How many students enjoy both rock and rhythm and blues, but not country-western?

Using Overhead Manipulatives

(Use with Lesson 12-7)

Permutations and Combinations

Objective Explore and use permutations and combinations.

Materials

- transparency pen*
- blank transparency cut into ten rectangular "cards"
- 2 blank transparencies

* = available in Overhead Manipulative Resources Kit

Demonstration 1
Permutations

- Ask three students to stand in a line at the front of the class. Tell the class that these three students represent a **permutation**, an arrangement of names, objects, or people in a particular order. Have the students change their order and tell the class that they now represent a different permutation of the same people. Have the students return to their seats.

- Write the numbers 1, 2, 3, and 4 on four transparency cards, one number per card. Ask a student to choose any three cards and place them in any order on the screen. Record the number formed on a transparency and label it *permutation*.

- Ask another student to use the same three cards to form a different number. Record this number.

- Continue rearranging the same three cards until all possible three-digit numbers have been recorded. Ask students how many numbers were formed. **6**

- Now use all four cards. Have students arrange the cards to form all the 4-digit numbers they can. Ask how many numbers were formed. **24**

- Show students the list of three-digit numbers they formed. Ask, "Can you see any way we could organize these numbers into groups?" **Sample answer: Make groups of numbers with the same first digit.**

- Show students the list of four-digit numbers they formed. Ask whether these numbers could be organized in a way similar to the three-digit numbers. **Yes; you can also group numbers with the same first and second digit.**

- Ask students to look for a way to predict the number of permutations from the number of digits. **Sample answer: For three digits, multiply 3 times 2; for four digits, multiply 4 times 3 times 2.**

- Ask whether the number of permutations of five digits would be greater than, less than, or equal to the number of permutations of four digits. **greater than**

- Ask students to predict the number of permutations for five digits. **120**

(continued on the next page)

Chapter 12

Demonstration 2
Combinations

- Clear the screen. Say "The next activity is a little different than the activity we just completed. When we are finished, we will compare them."
- Ask students to name six of their favorite toppings for pizza. Write each topping on a transparency card and place the cards on the screen.
- Tell students that they are going to order a pizza combining two toppings. Have a student select any two cards. Record the combination on a blank transparency.
- Ask another student to select a different combination of two cards. Record the combination on a transparency and label it *combination*. Repeat until all possible combinations of two toppings from the six possible toppings have been recorded. Ask students whether onions and mushrooms is the same combination as mushrooms and onions. **There are 15 different combinations; yes.**
- Repeat the activity making combinations of four toppings. **There are 15 different combinations.**
- Ask students to explain the difference between a combination and a permutation. **In a combination, order is not important; in a permutation, order is important.**

Extension
Real-World Examples
Ask students to name other examples of permutations and combinations. **Sample answers: permutation—electing one person as club president, one as treasurer, and one as secretary; combination—electing three members to be student council representatives**

Algebra Activity

(Use with Lesson 12-6)

Punnett Squares

Materials: integer mat, algebra tiles, counters

Use the materials to model a Punnett square with two traits. Use the tiles to represent one gene, and the counters to represent the other gene. Let the shaded tile and the shaded counter represent the dominant gene. Let the unshaded tile and the unshaded counter represent the recessive gene.

1. In this square, you are representing the offspring of peas. The traits are round or wrinkled, and yellow or green. Round and yellow are the dominant genes. Wrinkled and green are the recessive genes. Complete the Punnett square.

	R Y	R y	r Y	r y
R Y				
R y				
r Y				
r y				

2. What are the different combinations?

3. How many of the peas are round and yellow?

4. How many of the peas are round and green?

5. How many of the peas are wrinkled and yellow?

6. How many of the peas are wrinkled and green?

Chapter 12

Mini-Project

(Use with Lesson 12-9)

Verifying Probability by Experiment

Work in groups of 4. Do Exercises 5–12 individually and then combine results in Exercises 13–18.

The probability that something will happen is found by the rule

$$\text{probability} = \frac{\text{number of ways that an outcome can occur}}{\text{number of possible outcomes}}.$$

There are 6 possible outcomes when rolling a die. The probability of rolling a 1 is $\frac{1}{6}$. Use the probability rule to complete the chart below.

	Outcome	Probability
	1	$\frac{1}{6}$
	2	$\frac{1}{6}$
1.	3	
2.	4	
3.	5	
4.	6	

Roll a die 60 times for each number in the exercises in the table below. Tally and total the number of successes for each exercise.

	Outcome	Tally of Successes	Number of Successes
5.	1		
6.	2		
7.	3		
8.	4		
9.	5		
10.	6		

11. Did 1 come up $\frac{1}{6} \times 60$, or 10 times?

12. How often did you get a 2? a 3? a 4? a 5? a 6?

Record the results obtained by your group.

	Names of Students	1	2	3	4	5	6
13.							
14.							
15.							
16.	Your results						
17.	Total for four						
18.	Average						

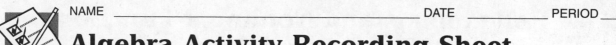

Algebra Activity Recording Sheet

(Use with the Lesson 12-9 Follow-up Activity on pages 656–657 in the Student Edition.)

Simulations

Materials: number cube, coin, 2 colors of counters, 2 colors of marbles

Activity 1

Use the table below to record your data.

Answers	T	F	F	T	T	T	F	F	T	F	Number Correct
Simulation 1	F	T	T	F	F	F	T	T	T	F	2
Simulation 2											
Simulation 3											

Analyze the Data

1. Based on the simulations, is tossing a coin a good way to take the quiz? Explain.

Extend the Activity

Use a simulation to act out the problem.

2b. Based on your simulation, how many meals must be purchased in order to get all six different prizes?

Activity 2

Record your results of the simulation in the chart below.

Misses the first shot	Makes the first shot, misses the second	Makes both shots

Record your answers for Exercises 3–8 on the back of this sheet.

Chapter 12

Polynomials and Nonlinear Functions
Teaching Notes and Overview

Algebra Activity Recording Sheet

Modeling Polynomials with Algebra Tiles
(p. 160 of this booklet)

Use With Lesson 13-1 as a follow-up activity. This corresponds to the activity on page 673 in the Student Edition.

Objective Use algebra tiles to model polynomials.

Materials
algebra tiles

Students use algebra tiles to model monomials, binomials, and trinomials. They also find the degree of polynomials.

Answers
See Teacher Wraparound Edition p. 673.

Algebra Activity Recording Sheet

Modeling Multiplication
(p. 161 of this booklet)

Use With Lesson 13-4 as a preview activity. This corresponds to the activity on page 682 in the Student Edition.

Objective Use algebra tiles to model the multiplication of polynomials.

Materials
algebra tiles

Students use algebra tiles to model and solve multiplication problems involving a monomial and a binomial. The extension activity asks students to model multiplication of two binomials.

Answers
See Teacher Wraparound Edition p. 682.

Mini-Project
Multiplying Binomials
(p. 162 of this booklet)

Use With Lesson 13-4 as an extension activity.

Objective Use algebra tiles to model and solve binomial multiplication problems.

Materials
algebra tiles

Students work in small groups to model the multiplication of binomials. They then write a rule for multiplying two binomials and use the rule to find products.

Answers

1. $x(2x + 1) = 2x^2 + x$

2. $3(2x + 1) = 6x + 3$

3. When combined together, the models in Exercises 1 and 2 make the model at the top of the page.

4. $x(2x + 1) + 3(2x + 1)$

5. Distributive Property; Distributive Property

6. Answers will vary. Sample: If $a, b, c,$ and d are terms of two binomials, then $(a + b)(c + d) = ac + bd + bc + bd$.

7. $2x^2 + 7x + 3$

8. $2x^2 + 13x + 15$

9. $4x^2 - 23x - 6$

10. $3x^2 - 2x - 1$

Using Overhead Manipulatives

Graphing Parabolas
(pp. 163–164 of this booklet)

Use With Lesson 13-6.

Objective Investigate graphs that are nonlinear.

Materials
coordinate grid transparency*
transparency pens*
compass*
graph paper
student compasses
* = available in Overhead Manipulative Resources Kit

- This demonstration shows students that not all equations in two variables result in graphs of straight lines. The teacher graphs points that form a parabola. A compass is used to make the arc connecting the points in order to show that the graph's distance from the focus and from the x-axis are the same.

- The extension activity asks students to decide how a parabola opening to the right would be different from one that opens up.

Answers
Answers appear on the teacher demonstration instructions on pages 163–164.

Algebra Activity Recording Sheet

(Use with the Lesson 13-1 Follow-up Activity on page 673 in the Student Edition.)

Modeling Polynomials with Algebra Tiles

Materials: algebra tiles

Model and Analyze

Use algebra tiles to model each polynomial.

1. $-3x^2$

2. $5x + 3$

3. $4x^2 - x$

4. $5x^2 + 2x - 3$

5. Explain how you can tell whether an expression is a monomial, binomial, or trinomial by looking at the algebra tiles.

6. Name the polynomial modeled below.

7. Explain how you would find the degree of a polynomial using algebra tiles.

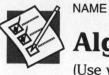

Algebra Activity Recording Sheet

(Use with the Lesson 13-1 Follow-up Activity on page 673 in the Student Edition.)

Modeling Multiplication with Algebra Tiles

Materials: algebra tiles

Model and Analyze

Tell whether each statement is *true* or *false*. Justify your answer with algebra tiles.

1. $x(x + 1) = x^2 + 1$

2. $x(2x + 3) = 2x^2 + 3x$

3. $(x + 2)2x = 2x^2 + 4x$

4. $2x(3x + 4) = 6x^2 + 4x$

Find each product using algebra tiles.

5. $x(x + 5)$

6. $(2x + 1)x$

7. $(2x + 4)2x$

8. $3x(2x + 1)$

9. Suppose there is a square garden plot that measures x feet on a side.

    a. Suppose you double the length of the plot and increase the width by 3 feet. Write two expressions for the area of the new plot.

    b. If the original plot was 10 feet on a side, what is the area of the new plot?

Extend the Activity

10. Write a multiplication sentence that is represented by the model at the right.

x^2	x^2	x	x	x
x	x	1	1	1
x	x	1	1	1
x	x	1	1	1
x	x	1	1	1

Mini-Project

(Use with Lesson 13-4)

Multiplying Binomials

Work in small groups.

In Lesson 14-6, you found the product of $x + 3$ and $2x + 1$ by using tiles as a model as shown in the figure at the right. The product is the sum of the areas of the tiles, that is, $2x^2 + 7x + 3$.

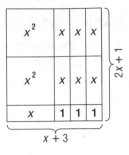

For each model, name the monomial and binomial being multiplied and give their product. Hint: Compare the models to the figure above.

1.

2.

3. Compare the models in Exercises 1 and 2 with the model at the top of the page. What do you notice?

4. Using Exercise 3, name the sum of the two products that equal $(x + 3)(2x + 1)$.

5. What property can you use to multiply x and $2x + 1$? to multiply 3 and $2x + 1$?

6. Write a rule for multiplying two binomials.

Use the rule you wrote in Exercise 6 to find each of the following products. Verify the multiplication using tiles. If necessary, adjust your rule. Remember to combine like terms in your answers.

7. $(x + 3)(2x + 1)$

8. $(2x + 3)(x + 5)$

9. $(x - 6)(4x + 1)$

10. $(3x + 1)(x - 1)$

Using Overhead Manipulatives

(Use with Lesson 13-6)

Graphing Parabolas

Objective Investigate graphs that are nonlinear.

Materials
- coordinate grid transparency*
- transparency pens*
- compass*
- graph paper
- student compasses

* = available in Overhead Manipulative Resources Kit

Demonstration
Graphing a Parabola

- Tell students that not all equations in two variables result in a straight line when they are graphed. Tell them that you are going to investigate a graph that is *nonlinear*.

- Display the grid transparency. You may want to have students follow along on graph paper at their seats. Graph and label the points $X(0, 2)$, $Y(-4, 4)$, and $Z(4, 4)$ using a black pen for the points and a blue pen for the labels. *Note*: Using a black pen to graph the points that lie on the parabola and colored pens to draw arcs, labels, and point F will help students see the curve suggested by the points plotted.

- Graph and label point $F(0, 4)$.

- Show students as you open the compass to a length of 6 units. Place the compass at F and draw an arc that intersects the grid line that is 6 units above the x-axis, on both sides of the y-axis. Graph and label the points of intersection P and Q.

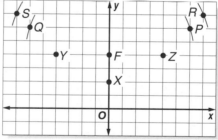

- Open the compass to a length of 8 units. With the compass at point F, draw an arc that intersects the grid line 8 units above the x-axis. Label the points of intersection R and S.

- Repeat this process to plot three more pairs of points.

- Ask students what figure the points graphed in color suggest. Show students as you use the black pen to sketch a smooth curve through the points. Tell students that the curve you sketched is called a **parabola**.
  a curve

(continued on the next page)

- For each point you plotted, ask students to compare its distance from the x-axis and its distance from point F. **The distance is the same.**

- Ask students whether they think each point on the curve can be described the same way. Choose any point on the curve and use the compass to compare its distance above the x-axis and its distance from point F. **yes**

- Ask students to state a definition of a parabola based on this activity. Point out that the line in this case was the x-axis. **A parabola is the set of points that are the same distance from a given point and a given line.**

Extension
Other Parabolas
Point out that the parabola you have drawn opens up. Ask students whether a parabola could be drawn that would open to the right. Ask them how drawing it would differ from the parabola they drew that opened up. **Yes; point *F* would be to the right of the bottom of the curve and the given line would be vertical.**